HERE, NOW

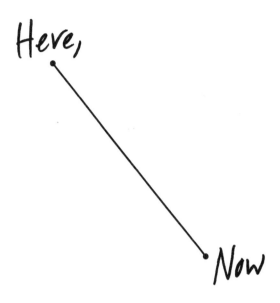

Here,

Now

ESSAYS

MICHELLE SUZANNE MIRSKY

Northwestern University Press
Evanston, Illinois

Northwestern University Press
www.nupress.northwestern.edu

Printed in the United States of America

10   9   8   7   6   5   4   3   2   1

Library of Congress Cataloging-in-Publication Data

Names: Mirsky, Michelle Suzanne, author.
Title: Here, now : essays / Michelle Suzanne Mirsky.
Description: Evanston, Illinois : Northwestern University Press,
    2024.
Identifiers: LCCN 2024021438 | ISBN 9780810147843 (paperback) |
    ISBN 9780810147850 (ebook)
Subjects: LCSH: Essays. | Parental grief. | LCGFT:
    Autobiographies. | Essays.
Classification: LCC PS3613.I78 A3 2024 | DDC 814/.6—dc23/
    eng/20240725
LC record available at https://lccn.loc.gov/2024021438

// For Joss. All of it; always. //

CONTENTS

HERE, AFTER.

I've been here before. In the crucible. Missing everything before. Longing for after. It's been ten years since my three-year-old son, Lev, died, very early on a Wednesday morning. November 3, 2010. Election Day was the day before; I don't remember it seeming important or even relevant that I vote that year. Lev died from a recurrence of lymphoma, suddenly but not unexpectedly, inside the state-of-the-art children's hospital where I worked. The hospital building sits on the site of the former Austin airport, high on a hill made from recycled crushed runways. I don't work there anymore. Seven years after Lev died, I had the opportunity to buy a tall, skinny house within eyeshot of the old air traffic control tower. I live here, now, inside the ghost airport, with my husband of two years and my teenaged son, who was not yet in kindergarten when his younger brother died. In 2020, the world shrank down and we three came to live our whole lives inside our little place. Online school, work-from-home, grocery shopping, three meals a day, masked dog-walks in loops around the block and up and down familiar streets. The zebrawood urn that holds Lev's ashes sits in the office on the ground floor, where I write, less than one mile from the hospital. In a few days, it will be Election Day. November 3, 2020. I took the day off from work even though I cast my vote early. So many reasons for sorrow and fear connected to this single day. Ten years. Four years. Voids and vessels. Prismatic days, whole years that bend the light away.

●————●

The first anniversary of Lev's death is a blur. The world wobbles on its axis from the weight of my pain and I am seasick with knowing. My mother is in town to spend time with me and my living son, and to shield him from my grief for a few hours. I take the day off work. I get a tattoo.

I drink whiskey. I meet an idol. I'm always in love. My heart is on the outside of my body, bruised and screaming.

On the second anniversary, I have brunch with new friends and take my seven-year-old to a music festival. I don't tell anyone about the significance of the day. We ride back to our car in a pedicab wearing our giveaway sunglasses at night. When we get home, I put my sleepy kid to bed and I sob in my room for a long time. On the sixth of November 2012, we reelect Obama. I make white bean soup while I watch the returns come in. In 2013, Election Day and Lev's third deathiversary pass like ships in the night. I go to a burlesque show. I forget to vote. The next year, on the fourth anniversary, I turn forty, I vote early for Wendy Davis, I don't write anything about Lev on social media. The fifth anniversary of Lev's passing is a Tuesday, Election Day, 2015. There are no candidates on the ballot in Texas. I don't vote. My dearest friends throw me a dinner party at a house I am about to move into, but which, at the time, has just a few odd pieces of furniture and not even enough chairs for all of us to sit at the table. We stoke the fire in the fire pit in the backyard and drink red wine. Everything is possible.

Nothing is off the table. I've lived five years beyond my own Viking funeral and the worst is behind me. I am certain the unknowable future is brighter than anything I've seen yet. I write: *Five years ago, we lost Lev. He was half of my whole heart and everything went black. It took me some time to regather the puddles and piles of love that spilled out of the wounds grief left on me. But I've got it now. I've got all the love. Come at me . . .*

A few weeks before Election Day 2016, I leave my job at the hospital. It feels equally like stepping off a cliff and like walking on air. I watch the election coverage on TV, flipping between channels, and like everyone in the entire world, I do not see Trump's win coming. Until it comes. And the sea change is surprisingly instant. The veil is peeled all the way back. At my son's hockey game the Sunday after, I am as yet grieving the future. Going through the motions. At the rink, I look up from my own shocked sadness to see lively parents in fleece vests and cowboy boots, gleeful, celebrating, not a care in the world. It's at this moment that I realize grief, applied as a lens, will show you things you wouldn't otherwise see. My grief is Rowdy Roddy Piper's sunglasses in *They Live*. It lets me see clearly these fellow hockey parents are aliens who voted for the weird, orange monster. I can see everything but there's nothing I can do about it. Dining out a few weeks later, I overhear white Republicans at an adjacent table talking loudly and proudly about teaching their college-aged daughters to carry guns in their vehicles in order to protect themselves from the residents of neighborhoods near where we live.

I start a new job in Public Health three weeks after the 2016 election. Two months later, I march on the Texas State Capitol with thousands of other women. I have a conversation with the lady butcher at my local grocery store about what the hell is even happening. Everything in the whole world has gone crazy, she says.

In the spring of 2017, I buy the house in the airport. My boyfriend lays down new floors. He moves in the following year. For his fortieth birthday, in August 2018, I have his favorite cake shipped in dry ice from New York City to Austin, Texas. I order giant Mylar balloons from Party City, and when I drive to pick them up, I listen to Tori

Amos and sing at the top of my lungs with tears streaming down my face the whole way. Something is coming. We get engaged the next month, my fifteen-year-old dog dies the month after that, and on Election Day 2018, the blue wave sweeps a Democratic majority into the US House. Eleven days after the year turns over into 2019, we get married. A planned elopement at the Blanton Museum of Art. My son, two friends, and our photographer are the only witnesses as we make our vows quietly to one another under a rainbow pinwheel of light inside the otherwise-empty *Austin*, Ellsworth Kelly's posthumously constructed minimalist temple of color and white space. My only living child is thirteen on our wedding day, a proto-adult, lanky and elegant and unsure of his limbs, a newborn horse in a slim one-button gray Cary Grant suit, a borrowed YSL tie, and Vans. He hands us our rings.

On the Saturday after Thanksgiving, 2019, we leave on a week-long three-city tour of Japan—new husband, teenage son, and me. Looking back from now, the idea of flying twelve hours across oceans for fun feels like an artifact: torturous and amazing, all mixed up together, crowded into trains and underground shopping malls; packed shoulder-to-shoulder in restaurants; throngs of commuters and tourists moving in sync through intersections, bees in a hive—every person, every one of us, blissfully unaware of the spreading virus and worldwide sequester only weeks away.

In the waning hours of 2019, my husband and I are home after a big dinner at a favorite restaurant with old friends and a small New Year's Eve party at the home of newer friends. We are sober and sleepy, happy to be resting our forty-something bones before the year turns over. From my bed, a single firework sparkles in the stairway window. I stand and walk toward the light, now a panorama of twinkling color spreading across the midnight sky, low and bright bursts coming from absolutely everywhere, like bombs in wartime. We live too far east to see the municipal fireworks on Town Lake from our house. These are just regular folks in their yards, making magic at midnight with explosives bought, more than likely, from a roadside stand somewhere just outside of town. Breathtaking and mundane. Welcome to 2020. No one has any idea what's coming.

Of all of the things I've done and lived through, raising a healthy teenaged son is the most challenging, the most devastating, the most hopeful. In March, after the city of Austin cancels SXSW but before businesses in Texas go dark, my son leaves on a long-planned spring break vacation with his best friend's family to the Texas Gulf Coast. They ride around in golf carts wearing Hawaiian shirts, meeting girls. After the kids return from the beach, the pandemic engulfs the world. Places of connection, places of contact, places of commerce shut down one after the other, far and wide and close to home. The streets are empty of cars, no one goes anywhere. My son finishes the school year online. It does not go well, but it doesn't matter. It's fine. Everyone in my neighborhood takes up jogging or remembers they own a bike.

When the pandemic hits, I'm in my fourth year supervising a team in the vaccine unit of the local health department. Like everyone, I begin working from home full time. My staff and I adjust to seeing one another only in little tiled windows inside our laptop screens. We learn to use Zoom and Microsoft Teams. We meet—virtually—which sounds futuristic but is mostly just awkward. Health department supervisors and managers in the post–hurricane Katrina era go through in-depth training on how to lead a multi-agency emergency response. We practice these skills in tabletop exercises. When natural disasters hit Central Texas, we organize shelters and supplies. Not one of us has lived through a worldwide pandemic. This is new to everyone. We are making it up in real time.

A few weeks into the COVID-19 shutdown, hospitals worldwide are filled with more and sicker people than the infrastructure can possibly handle. There's no treatment. No vaccine. My boss's boss calls me in to help with emergency response. I'm to serve as one of the rotating Incident Commanders at a massive drive-thru COVID-19 testing site spun up in the parking lot of a graffiti-covered, condemned Home Depot. The command center for the testing operation is located in what used to be the garden center. Before the site opens to the public each day, the staff meets as a team under the glass of the former greenhouse, socially distanced & masked: about eighty folks pulled from a patchwork of city departments, medical staffing agencies, and local hospital groups. I lay out the plan for the day and make a motivational speech from behind my N-95 respirator. The scene is apocalyptic and uplifting and also deeply absurd. We take it as it comes, we make it up as we go along. We are grateful to have the chance to show up and be in community. To feel not alone. We take care of each other. We take nothing for granted.

During the months that I'm assigned to the response, I drive to work each morning on empty streets in the pre-dawn dark. The dormant city is never not shocking. The highways are only slightly less deserted in the blistering afternoon sun. At a stoplight on my drive home, the driver of the car next to me has a bandana pulled up over his nose and mouth. I think to myself: he's a bandit. A bank robber. Then I realize: no. Driving alone with my windows up and AC on blast, I too am wearing a mask. You can't be too careful.

The pandemic proves a pass-fail test for relationships, a furnace that smelts the ore of your joint raw material; you dissolve or you are buttressed. For my husband and me, the months spent sheltering at home during a global pandemic are some of the strongest of our five-year relationship. We nurture one another. We feather our nest. We rarely fight and, when we do, it's succinct, solved and over, nothing like before. When I'm not at the testing site, my husband makes coffee for both of us each morning, like always. I walk our new dog while the sunlight is still coming up pink and orange. He does the laundry, relishes vacuuming; I order the groceries, cook weekend breakfast and weeknight dinners. If we're home together all day, we text one another photos of our pets from different floors of the house. We spend too much money on take-out dinners from our favorite restaurants. There is a tranquility between us with which I am wholly unfamiliar in my life and relationships. I am content. I am so grateful. I have never been here before.

Inside my head, I prepare, always, for the fall, for the mess, for the nameless but certain catastrophe I know is coming. This is who I am. I am a knot of consuming worry—worry about the misfortunate state government of Texas where I live; worry about the thin veneer of safety in pandemic-rattled New York State, where I'm from—worry about the health of my elderly parents who live there, and whom I cannot travel to see; worry about voter suppression, about the ugliness of white supremacy that was always here but now parades proudly in the harsh light of day; worry about the devastating personal toll of this fucked-up time on people who were already struggling and on those who are suddenly drowning.

———

The 2020 presidential election between Joe Biden and Donald Trump happens on November 3. It's not a landslide. We wait for answers and nothing changes in the crucible. Conspiracy theories grow in the vacuum of uncertainty. People are hiding in their homes. Moving houses. Moving cities. People are desperate. People are dying.

In the last weeks and months of 2020, the Health Department anticipates the arrival of the COVID-19 vaccine with a series of clinics in public spaces, vaccinating for influenza as a stand-in for COVID. The last big practice run before the arrival of the COVID-19 vaccine is a massive drive-thru flu clinic at the County Expo Center, in a barn built for the rodeo. On the Saturday after Election Day, the emergency preparedness team, the entire immunization staff, and a baker's dozen of nurses report for work before sunup and work through the late afternoon. It's been months since this many of us have all been together in the same place, and the energy is intense. We're all used to wearing masks and shouting to bridge six feet of safe social distance. Over the lunch hour, the news hits our phones and spreads quickly: enough votes have been counted to officially declare Joe Biden the next president of the United States of America. We are mostly liberal here in this rodeo barn. A bunch of bloody hearts betting it all on the possibility of a better future. Some of us pause to high-five one another. Others to wipe tears of relief. The lot of us bending like sun-starved plants toward this pinpoint of political light in the long dark landscape we've been white-knuckling our way through.

The first shipment of COVID-19 vaccine arrives at the Health Department two days after Christmas 2020. We make a plan to vaccinate at-risk workers with the limited supply we receive. We call in nursing home workers, folks working in hot zones at COVID testing sites, volunteers supporting unhoused populations. There is a line out the door of people with appointments, all holding printouts of their emailed invitations, wanting to make certain there's no mistake. We have nurses on standby to handle anxiety attacks and vaccine reactions, which look exactly the same: people faint.

I spend New Year's Eve working Incident Command at a COVID-19 vaccine clinic inside a rec center in Northeast Austin. We vaccinate about a hundred people. One of the staff brings in frosted shortbread cookies in the shape of champagne flutes. We take little breaks to sit outside to eat them. Moments of unmasked joy. We're equal parts exhausted and slap-happy and glad to be of service. At the end of the night, we have a single vial with three leftover doses and no one waiting to be vaccinated. We round up the security guard. A library manager. When we offer to vaccinate the custodian with the final dose, he balks: Is it okay? Is he allowed? Someone else must need it more. We tell him: This is your lucky day, sir. This one is yours. He nods. Agrees. His smile as the nurse prepares to vaccinate him telegraphs relief, terror, gratitude—exactly what all of us are feeling at the end of this extraordinary 365 days. Happy Fucking New Year. 2020 is finally done with us.

———

A couple of months into the pandemic lockdown, I'm digging in my purse, looking for my recently filled Rx of higher dose antidepressants. Buried at the bottom of my bag, I find the red suede half-moon zipper pouch full of my favorite lipsticks. Without opening the tubes, I know the four shades of bright red, one coral orange, and three rosy nudes by heart. I dump them out and turn their shiny black plastic and cool gray metal cases over in my palms. I think:

I miss fancy dress-up dates. I miss telling stories on stage. I miss trips together before we were married, New Orleans and Paris and Baja California Sur. I miss mini-breaks in fancy hotels with our elderly dog, who lived a long life. I miss wandering Brooklyn, shopping and stopping for champagne and oysters, madly in the beginnings of love; I miss watching Hitchcock on the big screen, day-drinking whiskey and eating cheese plates; I miss driving home at 2 a.m. on a Tuesday after an open-mic, belly full of late-night food truck Chicken Kara-Age. I miss being packed shoulder to shoulder inside general admission music venues, sweaty and irritated at all of the tall men in front of me. I miss parties. I miss lingering hugs with new loves. I miss all of the apartments I lived in that never felt like home. I miss panic attacks that came on like freight trains. I miss the pendant full of my son's ashes that I lost in a hotel in D.C. on the morning I was flying home. I miss the friendships I ended and the friendships that were ended for me. I miss the babies of friends who I never got to meet, who have since grown into surly adolescents. I miss singing to my own babies, rocking them to sleep in their bedroom in my long-ago dream house in the arm shell rocking chair that moved with me to each temporary resting place and now sits idle and ornamental, a design element in my living room.

I miss the tip of Cape Cod, the dunes and the ocean and the seaweed, fried clams and drag queens. I miss driving the streets of Hollywood and Silverlake and Santa Monica, mixtapes on actual cassettes in my blue jellybean car, Fiona Apple and Ivy and Cat Power and Elvis Costello and Common and Van Morrison pouring from the open windows sailing down Fountain, down La Cienega, down Pico. I miss dancing at the Dragonfly in a brand-new century, a whole new millennium, three or four of us crammed into a bathroom stall, bumps of cocaine until our hearts felt like they would explode, spilling out onto the sidewalk, breathless, watching my friends smoke cigarettes, waves of sparkling joy rolling off of all of us.

I take a breath, put the lipsticks back in their case, and zip it up; toss it back into the archive of my life before. Whatever's coming next will be here soon.   But also.   There is an after.

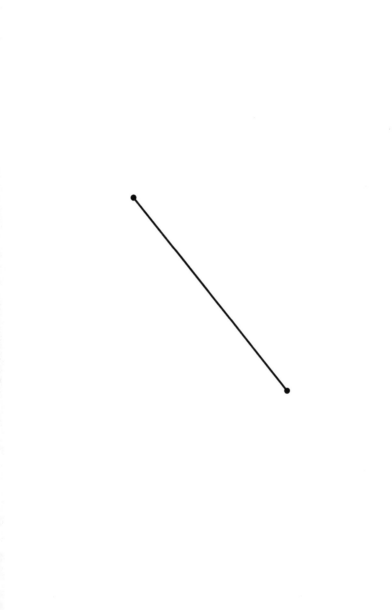

THESE THINGS HAPPENED

In the space of my darkest year, in no particular order, these things happened. My younger son died. My marriage ended. A rabbi and renowned jazz musician whom I'd only met once performed my son's funeral. People applauded. I fell in love with a blond poet suffering from PTSD. It didn't work out. My divorce was granted. The only Jewish funeral director in town admitted to me, unbidden, that her life's passion is improv comedy. My ex-husband threatened my boyfriend's balls via Facebook. I fled—and sold—my dream house. My older son lost his first tooth and entered kindergarten. I performed stand-up comedy. People applauded. I fell in love again. I realized I'm not afraid of anything.

In corporate America, businesspeople go on Outward Bound adventure retreats to try to be better at annihilating their competition through the conquest of rock walls or to learn to excel at firing people via the exhilaration of zip-lining across a ravine. For me, living through four years of being waterboarded by life afforded me the skills to be better at everything. I can't track how one event led to another. That's not the point. The point is this: the crucible in which I found myself during my darkest year had everything to do with my not giving a fuck about fear any longer. Don't mistake my lack of fear for lack of feeling. I cry so often that sometimes I don't even realize I'm crying until the tears on my laptop make the mouse work funny. Not a day goes by that I don't find myself gut-punched in the gaping hole left by my son's death.

From the moment before Lev was born when we found out that he had serious heart defects—and named him after the Hebrew word for heart (Lev is also Russian for "lion")—until he died suddenly in the wee hours of a Wednesday in November, I lived for this kid. I lived to overachieve at being his mother. I lived to make sure I knew more about his staggeringly complex medical self than anyone else, even more than the doctors. I lived to make sure he always had his favorite food or book or movie or shirt at the ready. I lived to administer IV medication three times a night at home so he could sleep in his own bed instead of in the cancer unit. I lived to puzzle over adding pureed veal to fruit smoothies so he could have clean protein. I lived to watch an endless loop of *The Muppet Show* and make it all okay when we were trapped in the hospital for months at a time. I lived on adrenaline, caffeine, and hospital cafeteria pizza. I stopped sleeping. I stopped writing. I stopped hoping for anything. I learned to speak the language of actuaries, of Medicaid administrators, of people with advanced degrees in medicine and nursing. I spoke the language of motivational speakers, of chaplains, of grief counselors and spiritual healers. Still, I began to have, in the confusion of early morning snooze-button half sleep, guilty dreams of airports, of flying, of leaving. And despite all of it, my hilarious red-haired three-year-old son died. He took a deep breath and he died.

It's a keen irony that the one thing at which I was exceptionally talented in this life was being the mother of this child who is gone. And the talent lay not only in navigating the complexity of his illness but in intuiting what this rare bird might need, because he was nothing like me or his father or anyone I'd ever known. It was like learning to raise an endangered species. This child, as a personality, as a companion, was incredibly easy. He knew how to make a stranger feel immediately comfortable. He could gauge a sense of humor and put anyone at ease. He grasped not just the timing, but the value of a good fart joke before he was old enough to speak. He was the instant best friend of everyone who met him. And I was his mother. I was the keeper of the awesome.

Since Lev was born, and since he died, my older son, Joss, has been a beacon in the fog. Joss is a lot like me, which is to say he's neurotic and abstract and sensitive. He has a dark sense of humor. There have been times since Lev's been gone that the only reason I've gotten out of bed at all was because Joss needed something. One day in the winter, after Lev died, Joss built a pillow fort around me in my bed when I couldn't stop crying.

The all-crying days have grown fewer and farther between. We are simpatico, Joss and I. Parenting him has largely been an exercise in humility and sighing and trying to stay a step ahead of a tiny male version of my own id. With Lev, I felt no such kinship. Instead, I felt something like total bafflement as to how I got so lucky. Seems absurd, throwing around the word "lucky" given that the boy had multiple heart surgeries as an infant, was diagnosed with a rare brain tumor at two, and eventually died at three from cancer that had spread throughout his body—but it's genuine. Everyone who knew him was fucking lucky and they knew it.

The morning Lev died we lay in his hospital bed together. I held onto his foot. His dad held his hand. There was nothing I could do to help him or to save him. There can be nothing worse than that feeling. That experience was the worst thing that could ever and will ever happen to me. So what else should I fear? What would you fear?

He died, and then he smiled. I recognize, realistically, it was some process of decay that produced that smile. But metaphorically, it felt like a tiny middle finger to the universe—the last laugh. It was Lev reminding everyone that he would always be the funniest one in the room. It was grotesque. It was perfect. Lev's sickness, his dying, the toll it took on everyone who knew him, was abjectly awful. I can't make it less so. And I can only spend so much time in the deep sea where all of this awful dwells. The rest of the time, I'm fishing in the shallows.

In the hours after Lev's death, I was consumed with making the transition from grieving the presence of Lev—his suffering, his pain, the worry—to grieving an absence: the absence of my beautiful boy. But I realized somewhere during that first day, the absence is not a void, but a vessel. It's a vessel that's mine to fill with wonder and experiences and joy for the rest of my life. And THAT is an incredible gift. Originally, I imagined the vessel as a cup, a vase, a bowl—something with an edge to overflow. But now, I see the vessel as a great cargo ship with Lev as its captain, sailing the sea, peering through a spyglass, looking for the next destination, the next treasure. Watching. Keeping me from wrecking on the rocks. This is where Lev lives for me.

My vessel, thus far, is filled with men and jokes. Both satisfy my need to plumb the middle depth between the sparkle of the surface and the blackness of the deep water. In sex and stand-up, there's a letting go, a desire to float, to dive but not drown. The first time I stepped onstage to tell jokes, I clicked into the rhythm of the crowd and began to figure out what they liked. It was not unlike a seduction. To have great sex is to excel at connecting on one very specific, very important, level. To excel at comedy, you need to make something like that connection with an entire crowd. You need to be in the moment together, feeling the adrenaline and endorphins and chemistry. When I'm performing, there's no propriety. I'm no one's ex-wife or grieving mother. It's not about my insecurities or personal failures or indulging my anxiety about the future. I mean, unless, of course, there's a joke there. Then, I'm going for it.

Obviously.

MY REAL PASSION IS
IMPROV COMEDY

Each day is allotted twenty-four hours, no more no less. In spite of this, around suffering and death, time goes elastic. Even as it's happening, you know it can't be right. Days when things seem more or less okay are bright confetti catnaps, papery and light; brisk, filmy collages of favorite things scented with salt air and snow and cooking smoke. Snap your fingers and they're over. Days when the big-bad is nigh become dark expanses like dying stars imploding in real time, roaring like a gun blast next to your ear and the sound hurts in your eyes and everywhere. So impossibly long as to seem without end. The ten days beginning with my thirty-sixth birthday were a jumble of these two sorts—alternating dim and manic and each pregnant with the end and the beginning of all things possible.

Day 1. I'd meant to be in Barcelona. Or at the very least in Houston, from where Lev and I had just returned sooner than expected. The second opinion of the world-class doctors there was medium-grim. Lev's prognosis is shaky as ever, but not anything we'd not recovered from at some other point in his life, right? Right. I'm crying this night, but not because my son is sick. I'm crying because the man I've been seeing for nearly a year has forgotten my birthday and I'm not getting laid and I'm pissed. I'm pissed in that way where all you can do is sputter and wail and clutch at pillows and fistfuls of tissues. As I cry, I uncover infinitely more and better reasons to cry, and I cry for those too. I let myself sink into it and really wallow. Because I know. This is it. I'm done. Lev's done. It's all done. Fuck it.

Day 2. Joss flies back from Arizona with a shitty cartoon-guy Halloween costume in his suitcase. I tease his hair into some rendering of this anime character he shows me on the package and we go trick-or-treating in our old neighborhood. I spend my first night with Joss in over two weeks. It feels like not enough.

Day 3. In the ICU with Lev. Draft break-up email to guy who forgot my birthday. Talk at length with Lev's doctors. Rewrite break-up email. Talk to more and different doctors. Rewrite email again. Skip my writing class. Hit send on email. Wait. No response. I'm there with Lev for the night. He's not sleeping well. I'm tired and exasperated and I wish I could fix it. I can't.

Day 4. The nurse taking care of Lev on Tuesday has known him literally his entire life and has never been one to get frantic. This day she endlessly wipes the sweat from her upper lip and tries not to curse under her breath while implementing the rapid-fire changes ordered one after another after another by Lev's doctors to try and stabilize him. They're sure he'll declare himself in a few days and we'll know if it's reversible. This time, though, the doctors insist we need to make decisions about whether to let him go if things go haywire. At a conference table with all of the doctors, I announce, naively, that my mother's instinct tells me it's not over. That he isn't done. It isn't time. I'm not worried. On Friday, Lev was laughing and talking and charming everyone in Houston. I'm thinking, how could this time—with his hair back and fiery, with his words back and hilarious, with everything so beautiful— how could this be his death throe?

His dad and I hold it together. We take a walk and we decide. On this day, we decide together that if and when Lev's body tells us it's ready to give up, we'd let him be ready. We aren't ready. We'll never be ready. But we would let him go if he told us he was ready. And he did. That night.

That night, I was supposed to go home to Joss. Twice I tried to leave, but Lev asked me not to go. Maybe he knew. I don't know. Around 9 p.m., something happened. An "event." Every alarm rang, the room filled with doctors and nurses and panic. Lev had declared himself. Lev was dying. This was it. And when they asked, we told them what we'd decided. And the doctors and nurses who'd cared for Lev his entire life had to shift from saving him to supporting him—and us—as he died. They had to make it okay for us, for themselves, to lose this child who had become family to them over three years of growing well and sick and well again in some or another unit of that hospital. And they did a beautiful, poetic job. They supported him with oxygen and morphine, made him comfortable, moved his crib out and a big bed in so we could lie with him. There were drinks and food on a cart. There was silence and peace and space to fall apart. We called our mothers and we told them Lev was dying. They each came to say goodbye, trading out with one another while the other kept watch over sleeping Joss. The nurses from the cancer unit came down and wept with us, held our hands, and went back to caring for children who were not dying that night.

Day 5. Lev hung on through the dark part of the night. At one point, he woke up and asked for water and talked to me for a minute. I don't remember what he said. I wish I could remember what he said. As the hours wore on, he slipped farther away into his morphine drip, but it was night, and he should have been sleeping, so it felt right. At about 5 a.m., I walked over to the couch to rest for a moment and I felt the nurse stir my leg and she said: It's time. It's happening.

And I crept over to the bed where his dad was cradling him, holding his hand. And I held his leg and his foot and he took a gasping breath and he was gone. The instant when the life of a person is gone from them is palpable. Every bit of energy left the room. No one even tried to make us move for what seemed like hours, but must have been minutes. Dozens of the nurses and doctors who'd cared for Lev came to his room and paid tribute to this baby like you would a politician lying in state. The stream of mourners was continuous until the colors were gone from the sky and the light was clear and blue and bright outside the window.

In the end, we were in the room with Lev for nearly seven hours after he died. I couldn't stop kissing his marble-cold forehead. We met a rabbi and a funeral director. Someone made the call to have Lev moved to the funeral home where he'd be cremated. The chaplain came and told me a story about a friend of hers who had died and who visited her as butterflies. Someone brought Joss to the hospital to see me in a playroom outside the ICU. He asked if Lev would be a zombie or a ghost or if he'd see his skeleton. It all seemed normal. Joss wanted to go to preschool so someone took him there. The rabbi—a stranger until that morning—who came, at the behest of a treasured physician friend, to console and to guide us, walked me to my car, waited while I sent a text message, and watched me set out alone. When I got to my house, all I wanted in the world was to throw out every scrap of Lev's sickness. So I pulled it out of every drawer, box, cabinet, and the grandmothers took it all away. I went through piles of paper, piles of clothes, piles and piles of piles. I pulled everything out of where I had hoarded it. And I made them throw it away. My dad dismantled the crib at some point. Everything must go. Everything.

That night, at the apartment, my mom woke up in a panic from a nightmare and I thought she was dying too. I called the paramedics and I followed the ambulance to the hospital. It was 3 a.m. before they let me take her home.

Day 6. Lev's dad had made plans for us to sit together with the Jewish funeral director and make the necessary arrangements. I put on a pretty blouse and makeup for some reason. And I strode in there like I was being interviewed by the media. At some point, there was coffee. We chose the urn and discussed the sort of service the rabbi might perform, and she awkwardly suggested how much we should pay him.

The funeral director listened to us tell stories about Lev's humor and recounted what others who'd known him had told her about him. She said aloud what we all were thinking—above all, the deceased was a funny kid. And then she paused as if to say something important. So we sat forward and listened intently. And she said: "I feel like we've shared a moment here, talking about your son Lev. Something wonderful. And I'd like to share something with you. I feel like I can do that. Because of Lev." And we were right there with her. And she continued: "The work I do is, obviously, incredibly serious. And over the years, I've needed an outlet. And I have developed a passion, which I think you'll appreciate." We nod. "And that passion." A pause. "Is improv comedy. I perform in an improv comedy troupe. I've never shared this with anyone. But I feel, because of Lev and how funny he was, I felt that I had to share it with you." Holy shit. Lev just made his first visit. And he brought gag gifts.

Later that day, while on my way to buy new boots for the funeral, I was approached by a depressingly clean-cut panhandler. Instead of my usual side-eye, I gave him a ten-dollar bill I had in my pocket. He asked, startled: "Are you sure?" I nodded and mumbled that I'd had a hard couple of days and wanted to pay some happy thing forward. He asked if he could pray with me and I—the atheist—nodded again. He took my hands and he prayed aloud that he didn't know what had happened in my life, but he prayed that it would get better. And as the light changed and I turned the corner into the plaza where the Nordstrom Rack awaited me he said: "I just know it'll all be okay for you, ma'am. Do you know of any jobs in construction?"

I parked the car, dropped my keys into my purse, and I wondered where the fuck I got a ten dollar bill. And then I remembered: In my sorting rampage that morning, I had pulled it out of a long-forgotten birthday card someone had sent Lev. Lev wanted to make sure I didn't spend his birthday money on trashy boots. Good for him.

I've theorized that maybe the weight of a day, the length of the sprawl of any given twenty-four hours is connected to its peculiarity—which part you can't process. You hold on to every bit of incomprehensible data in hope that you'll someday find the decoder ring and make sense of it. You keep only the Cliff's notes of the mundane days and you hoard the encyclopedic catalog of rarities and oddities. Except for a hail of bright fragments, though, I cannot remember the day of Lev's funeral, which was, without question, a day of epic strangeness.

Day 7. Like snapshots pinned to a clothesline, I can rearrange the images of this day a thousand times and never fill in the space between. I know what I wore (gray jacket, black skirt, black boots). I remember listening to the Black Keys' "Everlasting Light" in the car on the way to the funeral home. I remember Lev's dad clutching my arm as the rabbi spoke, helping me stand. Helping me not fall. I remember afterward, sitting in my backyard in the sunlight. Someone hands me Scotch. I remember hugging the heart surgeon in his beautiful suit in my kitchen. There were pink frosted cupcakes in a white box. Joss is wearing a striped jacket. When I hold him close, he's fuzzy and warm. I remember my girlfriends sitting very near to me, touching me all of the time, carrying me on their wings as if I were a baby bird. I remember eating sushi at happy hour. I remember a cocktail, a French 75, at a bar later in the evening. And a hooker. And a taco. And I remember laughing. I must have gone to sleep at some point. But I don't remember where I slept. I don't remember the day ending or beginning. Why can I make the detail knit together for Lev's death, but not for his funeral?

•————•

A few days later, after being told by another friend that he is frantic, I will reunite with the man who forgot my birthday. We will cry all afternoon in bed, warm together. I will miss an appointment to get my hair cut. That's all I remember. It's enough.

"IT'S ALL GONNA BREAK . . ."

My month with the Blond Poet was, on the surface and in all other ways, a terrible idea. Two hopelessly broken writers in the midst of ending marriages start frantically screwing between poetry readings and art shows. "You're in trouble," said the injured poet, his bruises still visible. "I'm trouble for you. I don't want to, but I'll hurt you . . ."

And I, the grieving mother, replied: "Well, don't hurt me, then. You don't have to, you know." No way was this ever going to end well.

The night I meet the poet, it has been one week to the day since Lev died. With the mourners mostly gone, I've begun to feel convalescent, frayed. I'm still on leave from work, alternately sleeping all day and climbing the walls. I accept all invitations. I arrive late to this reception on the roof of an art space downtown (the elevator plays a video loop of "The 900 Number" by the 45 Kings, interpreted into sign language). I am so hungry, but have missed the food. My friends feed me wine instead. A girlfriend has arranged to introduce me to this poet, having shown me a photo of him on her iPhone a month earlier. In the photo, he stood in a dressing room, a bearded blond in a light blue suit. The pants of which were, it could be argued, much too tight. When we meet in November, the poet is wearing a winter vest and dirty gray jeans. A season has passed. He is handsome despite the stitches in his lip and scrapes on his arms, the result of a bike wreck in which a car hit him and he went flying—his second serious accident in a year. He has no sense of humor about this. The night on the roof, his eyes keep finding the part of my leg between tall boot and short skirt.

The poet doesn't laugh at my jokes on the roof, but he's listening. When he smiles, his expression reads as suspension of disbelief. Some drunk twenty-something girl the poet knows spills a full glass of red wine into my purse. Everything is soaked. She doesn't apologize, keeps talking about semiotics and fashion. Her boyfriend rolls his eyes. I excuse myself to the restroom and throw away most of the contents of my purse. I try to shake the wet warmth out of my head, but it's mingled with the cold and I am fog. My legs erupt in goosebumps from sitting on the roof for too long, and from meeting you. You're blond; have a beard; are a poet. You're tall and indignant. You have watched me this whole night. You have kept up. You are mine, like a mink cape I want badly enough to steal from the coat check. I think all this, I try to sop it up but the wine has soaked into everything.

It gets cold and late and some of us move across the street to a restaurant with cowhide pillows and a fireplace and drink more red wine. In the lounge of the restaurant, I show the poet three of my tattoos. Later, he tells me this moment is when he knows he'll see me naked. Afterward, while we wait for the valet to bring our cars around, I touch his stomach with the palm of my hand and I ask if he's kissed anyone yet with his busted lip. He says he hasn't, but he'd be game to try. I'll bet you would, I say. And I drive off. Or at least that's how it happens in my head.

The next time we meet, everyone plays Threes at a dance party in a printmaker's studio. People have their own dice. One girl has fingerless gloves. It's legit. Everyone looks French or bohemian or East Coast preppy. I win some money, lose it again, and make an excuse to drive the poet and his bike home (he doesn't have or want his own vehicle, content to keep bouncing off cars indefinitely, it would appear). We spar about music all the way to his place. He says my favorite New Pornographers song is not the best. The best, he says, is on *Twin Cinema*. He can't remember what it's called. We should go inside and he'll play it for me. To which I reply: "What are we, fifteen?" But I go with him. "Sing Me Spanish Techno." Yeah, that's a good one. We make out on the couch in his freezing house with no heat till our lips hurt, and I'm fairly certain I eat his stitches at some point.

There's an abundance of research out there around grief and loss—some dry and some colorful—that points to sex as solace. This holds up mostly for men, who (per the research) typically intellectualize their pain and look for physical release in the wake of sorrow. Women are deemed "feelers." I don't exactly know what this means. What I do know is this: sex with the poet was like meth and opium stirred into a bottomless glass of warm milk; intense comfort after which I could not sleep. Too much was never enough. Morning: he would kiss me awake and we'd tear each other limb from limb, he'd make me coffee with honey and trace his fingers on my shoulders while I drank it. In between sips, I'd rest the mug on his divorce papers. Noon: we'd hide under heaps of blankets, warm and rushed. Night: he'd bring glasses of water and wine to bed for us, help me off with my boots and we're back under the covers, not sleeping.

We carried on a nonstop, rambling intellectual conversation that never became an argument, never a debate. Me: "Semantics is my God." Him: "Semantics never saved anyone. Except Bill Clinton." The rapport was fast and strong and natural—which, in turn, made us both uneasy. It was not a good idea for two people as broken as we were to get too relaxed. The worst was yet to come for each of us and we both knew it. In the meantime, we were busy drinking Malbec and eating fancy cheese and warm olives. He tells me one night as he opens the car door for me that he's trying to impress me. I tell him I'm impressed. We are like younger versions of ourselves. New. He touches me constantly. He cannot watch me across a table, on adjacent stools, sitting quietly, without grabbing some part of me and us falling. Words fail me. I say things anyway. I think: I want to memorize him and text him to my friends. I think: I love him. One night while he was dressing to leave, I buttoned his shirt for him like we were a couple of settled old folks. He smiled. Kissed my face. I scratched his beard.

The company of the poet and his cadre of art-makers made me anxious that I wasn't writing, that I had strayed so far from what I'd always done. So I wrote. At first I edited old stories. Then I started reworking abandoned ideas in a new voice. The poet was encouraging. He never asked and I never offered to let him read anything of mine. He woke early each morning and wrote before biking to his office. I preferred to write at night. If we'd not spent the night together, he would text or call me first thing to check in and I'd rouse myself, join the world. A routine. Like clockwork. I wrote, now. Again.

•————•

There is this kind of construction crane—the sort you have to get a whole crew of skilled workers to assemble before you can build the thing you needed the crane to lift into being. These cranes are stories tall and when they begin to take shape, they appear sturdy, permanent. And as you watch one getting built, you think you're watching an end unto itself, but it's the making of the means. The moment when the crane-not-structure realization hits you is confusion, longing, recalibration of expectations and a little bit of awe. I recount this analogy at lunch one day with the poet. We pull apart our grilled salami sandwiches and wipe grease from our fingers as we talk. Building these things—this marriage, this home, this family—and then dismantling them: my life thus far has been spent building a crane I needed to build the life I was building all along. He says all women want everything to turn into something, to evolve. But I don't think he's right. He tells me that he's moving to the East Coast (he doesn't). I feel like maybe I shouldn't see him again (I do).

After he watches the ghost of a drunk John Berryman being interviewed on the BBC, the poet lets his beard grow like rambling weeds for weeks. He tells me about Berryman over breakfast one Saturday morning. My broken cell phone calls my ex-husband and leaves this conversation on his voicemail. The poet's not-blue eyes are deep and wet. He tries to tell me he's breaking down. I try to hear him, but I can't help. I'm not here to help. He writes lines of poetry about my hair, my skin, my tattoos, and texts them to me. I watch him read forty of his poems (none of them are about me) on a stage at a bar. That night, I predict it. The End.

Me: You'll read me like a book, till you're sure know the story. Then you'll put me back on the shelf and not open me again.

Him: No, not like that.

Me: You'll see. I'm the poem that wrote you.

Him: Go to sleep, little girl. [*snore*]

The End, after so much banging, is all whimper. The poet breaks up with me via text message because he doesn't want to help me move my car. He immediately starts sleeping with a twenty-three-year-old blond cheerleader from the Midwest. There is talk—among our mutual friends—that he has had a minor breakdown, an after-effect of his bike wreck(s) et al., and he simply couldn't handle the intensity. Maybe he just needed to fuck more and new people to solve his ontological despair. It doesn't matter. We never spoke again. Not one time ever. That was it. Fin.

In the winter, months after we are done, I buy his new book—a book he was putting the finishing touches on when we met. I preordered it the first week it was available and hoped that in the months I'd have to wait for it to arrive from his small press, I'd finish pining, sober up. When the time came, it took me by surprise. I had been home a week with the flu. Chills and shakes and hallucinations. The first day I could get out of bed, I went to the mailbox and the book was there in a hand-labeled envelope. I read it cover to cover. Cried. Sobbed, really.

At its core, the book is about deciding to leave comfort behind, and then upon burning bridges, changing everything, starting a new life—realizing the new life is just as deadened and even more brutal, but you can't go home, because you belong nowhere when all is said and done. It's about divorce. It's about being an artist. It's about being in your thirties. It's about all of these things or none of these things. And it is brilliant. It made me feel better, somehow, that of all of the things I had gotten wrong, he most certainly was not a shitty poet.

Months later I will run into him on the street. I am on a date with a tall, handsome inconsequential fellow who is holding my hand at the time. I see the poet but it doesn't register until he's passed me that I had actually just SEEN THE POET. I hear the friend who's walking with him call out my name, I turn around to look and I yell back, wave. We don't stop. We keep on, walking in opposite directions. The poet sees me too now. He looks haunted. I'm the ghost. Or at least that's how it happens in my head.

A CURE FOR THE
HUMAN CONDITION

Of the many fears I gladly shed in the wake of my son's death, I miss the relentless dread of disappointment the least. Had I realized the moment the fear left me, I might have raised a glass of something aged and expensive, made a big to-do. As it happened, the terror of disappointment left me so quietly that by the time I realized it was gone all that was left was to search my recollections for the moment when I gave up the ghost and became brave and new, the border between before and after. The instant when my existence was liberated from the orbit of disappointment's sun came in July a few days before what would have been Lev's fourth birthday. I'm sitting on the top step of the highest staircase in my parents' very tall house in upstate New York, the house in which I grew up. And I'm stewing in a cold soup of disaffection.

Even though he's been gone nearly eight months at this point, I've been dreading the approach of the day Lev officially won't get any older, the day he won't have a cake or presents or a celebration of making it to the next buoy. That day, I think, will make it all real. I remember Lev's first birthday party in the backyard of this house, cohosted with his "best friend," my dad, who turned seventy that same year. I think about Lev taking his first steps—at age almost-two—in the living room two stories down. I think about how it had felt the year before when Lev, then three and with defiant swirls of recently returned strawberry blond hair, was there in the house with me for the last time. I wouldn't have taken this summer trip down memory lane but for Joss, who I am delivering to his dad and grandma for a Hamptons vacation.

In this moment, I'm sitting a few steps away from my childhood bedroom and thinking about how I used to get the dry heaves from nerves the night before going to summer camp (and how Joss, who'll head to camp for the first time in a matter of days, is not at all nervous; not worried in the slightest). I'm thinking about how it felt to be a lovesick teenager in this house. And how it felt to explain to my parents that I was breaking up with the first man they thought I would marry, and the next one, and the one I did marry. And I think about the men in my life now, who are making me crazy—every last one of them—and giving me little in return. And I'm trying to decide what's next, what the fuck I'm going to do.

I'm sitting at the top of my parents' house and I'm reading, on the tiny screen of my smart phone, these words: "Nietzsche famously said, 'Whatever doesn't kill you makes you stronger.' But what he failed to stress is that it almost kills you. Disappointment stings . . ." The words are from Conan O'Brien's 2010 commencement address at Dartmouth College, a year after he was forced out of his job as the host of *The Tonight Show* and replaced by Jay Leno. The key takeaway of O'Brien's Dartmouth address was the idea that having your worst fears realized is—maybe—the best thing that could ever happen to you (except that it's still the worst). Of everything he'd learned from his Ivy League education, in life, through the cutthroat trials of show business, this platitude from Nietzsche contained the point Conan O'Brien wanted to drive home. That and "Disappointment stings." In addition to feeling tremendous empathy for this tortured giant ginger of a man who'd been disillusioned on a grand scale, I thought to myself: "WELL, FUCKING DUH."

Historically, for as long as I can remember, my relationship to disappointment was something like respect rooted in terror. Disappointment was the star around which my world revolved. Like the Little Prince, I lived alone on my planet (whose poles were marked at one end by the fear of displeasing anyone ever and at the other by the anticipation of being let down by everyone always). The sting of disappointment was forever hot in my cheeks and cold in my soul. Over the years I learned to imagine the worst and to gird myself against the impact of my own poor showing or the failure of others to meet my expectations. I learned to aim low in the hope that by not aiming for success I could—in effect—dodge failure. To that end, I moved thousands of miles away from my family (to evade their judgment of my unambitious career choices and oft-abandoned creative endeavors), I stayed in terrible romances to avoid the end (or worse: the beginning of something new, ripe with fresh potential for disillusionment). To put it plainly, I hid. But the years of living in the fishbowl of Lev's hospital room had put me under a microscope and made the idea of controlling my image—managing others' expectations of me—moot. Instead I put my head down and submitted to the next indignity.

That evening, while Joss played with my mom and his cousin, my brother and I had gone to see the documentary *Conan O'Brien Can't Stop*, about what was ostensibly O'Brien's darkest year. Although the reasons for our disenchantment were dissimilar, I felt an affinity with Conan O'Brien's openness about how much his downfall at NBC wrecked him. And I felt a sense of solidarity with O'Brien's decision to go bold with his next endeavor. When I got home from the movies, I ate great forkfuls of the Dartmouth speech till the plate was empty. And when I was done, I sat a bit stunned on that familiar staircase with my darkest year turning rapidly to light. I thought about what disappointment had meant for Conan O'Brien, an admittedly blessed and lucky man—a proudly self-effacing Harvard-educated comic legend. Ambitious, driven, at the top of his field, O'Brien was financially and creatively successful with a happy, robust family to love and support him. Disappointment came for him as it comes for all of us and it nearly killed his will to create. Maybe it stung worse for this man who—on the eve of his yearlong television blackout—famously urged America not to be cynical. He hadn't spent his whole life steeling himself for failure. For all his accolades, he was sucker-punched by disappointment. Conan O'Brien's unceremonious ouster from NBC (which, let's be honest, amounted to a forced paid vacation with limitless possibilities) sent him into a deep depression. I think I must have realized in that instant that disappointment is the passive-aggressive cousin of death. It's not something any one of us can avoid successfully. It will get every one of us.

I hadn't been afraid of death for a long time. I'd resigned myself to the infinite sleep when I was a teenager. I'd spent my early adolescence calculating the odds of Reagan or Gorbachev pushing the red button at any given moment, terrorized by the inevitable end. Odd as it may seem, the tense denouement of the Cold War coupled with my atheism (and related belief that there's nothing after this life) forced me to develop some coping skills around my own mortality. Disappointment stuck around, though, as a major driver. Given the attention I lavished on mental dry runs of every possible tragedy, I might have fancied myself prepared for Lev's death. If not prepared, I was at least more than familiar with that particular sad ending. I'd practiced this dance before. I prepared to be without Lev before I was ever with him. When we'd gotten the first diagnosis, when I was twenty-two weeks pregnant, the doctor had taken us into his office and told me that the kid growing in me was a boy whose heart had formed all kinds of backwards and that if we went to Kansas, we could legally terminate the gentle kicking in my midsection and my need for designer maternity jeans. We demurred on the late-term abortion, but after that kind of halftime show, the rest of the pregnancy was your basic gallows-walk. At the end of the road was complex surgery on an organ the size of a macadamia nut. I busied myself with plucking all negative scenarios from the galaxy of possible outcomes and making peace with them long before—or if—they were real.

In advance of Lev's birth, I favored superstition. I wouldn't sanction a baby shower. I didn't buy a crib or arrange the nursery. I left the world alone. I thought perhaps if no one saw him coming, if I didn't disturb anything, there would be less of a blast radius when the world exploded. As it happened, I gave birth to a perfect-looking baby and had to hand him over to be cut into pieces. When I left the hospital without him, my heart was shrapnel. And so Lev's life began.

At the end of his life, after heart surgery and brain surgery and cancer and respite, when Lev's disease returned with a vengeance and killed him inside of a month, my fear was the truss that restrained me when I might have reached for optimism. I made every attempt to extinguish hope where I found it as if it were contagious and might infect me. As he fought and we all fought with him, and after somehow always managing to right the flight path of the airplane in free-fall to which Lev's life had become analogous, we lost. During our final weeks with the little lion, my ewer of disappointment reached maximum capacity. I had done everything I could to keep disappointment and death at bay. But we were beaten.

The reign of disappointment wasn't over when the brightest star went dark. Lev's death began a series of *are you kidding me with this shit?!* humbling experiences: the realization of exactly how hard it would be to be divorced, to coparent Joss in separate houses, to move on; a real estate *Sophie's Choice*; online dating (!); befriending (and defriending) awful people who did not have my back. It was, to say the least, a crushing weight.

There was a period surrounding Lev's death when I thought perhaps I might die too. I was more or less indifferent to the thought. During Lev's final stretch in the hospital (three months all told), I lost my voice for several weeks—the result of a convulsing cough. I'd somehow dropped twenty-five pounds without trying (at Lev's funeral, I'd worn two jackets and a belt to disguise the fact that none of my clothes fit). Not infrequently, during this time, my heart would leap and flop in my chest and I'd feel as if I might black out. I'd go to my car, lie down till it passed. Part of me almost hoped an actual affliction had taken root and would quietly end me. My attempts to address normal activities of daily living in those weeks when I'd thought I was dying resembled that aspect of a dream when one tries to dial a phone and one's fingers behave like leaden sponges. Bills sat unpaid, I forgot to feed the dog. Joss went to visit his grandmother in Arizona. My hair grew dirty and took on bizarre shapes. And then Lev died. And I did not die. And that was that.

The vagaries turned concrete by Lev's death were staggering, but they were no longer terrifying question marks. I could grab these certainties by the balls and crush. I could lurch forward. Lev's illness was the force of gravity that kept me tethered to planet Terrifying Letdown. And after he died each course correction served to erode my fear of the next shitstorm. I'd swallowed a bitter horse-sized pill of disappointment and my fever had broken. I'd let the fear of it go so completely, it took an earnest question from a wise man to bring its absence to my attention. Of course it still stings when the plan goes kablooey. But the fear is no longer an out-of-control speedboat dragging me behind as I try to water ski. In fact, it was nearly drowning in all of it that saved me, made me fearless. Turns out, Nietzsche was right. And so was Conan O'Brien.

WHERE'S TOM PETTY FROM?

At a moment when the mire of my grief threatened to subsume me, I made the decision to seek delight. I set about entangling myself with a dazzling iconoclast whom I had known and admired for many years. He required no convincing. The beauty of the thing was that it fit into the cracks of my life and of his: lunches and late nights and weekend afternoon snacks. The awfulness of the thing was that it turned out we were very fond of one another. Awful mostly in that I was still married. He was also not single. And this relationship was never intended for the realm of fairy-tale endings. In its effort to escape the sad morass, my grief-bound heart had reached for distraction and instead found itself in the gulag of an infatuation so all-consuming, my world rang with the song of it like the white noise of the ocean in a shell. If love is a mixtape, infatuation is a broken record; a single song played at a deafening volume. When things get star-crossed enough, you start to live inside the lyrics, and sometimes, it seems not half bad. This is how it went with my iconoclast for a while. During these months, I followed the gospel of Neko Case: I did my best. I was made of mistakes.

Much of my time with the iconoclast was a bubble of Peter Pan hedonism: champagne cocktails, giggling, marathon naps, bootlegged 1980s TV comedies, and ohdeargod sex. I relished the chance to hide in the surface with him and not apologize for the joy I found there. Sometimes, we'd lie awake at night and drop our diving bells into the deep sea of sadness and longing and existential terror. We were godless and fearless and certain only that there was nothing more than this. We fought intensely about his intractability, my selfishness. He lectured. I pouted. Neko Case again: this time, I was a tornado. Devastation and whirling chaos mistaken for love.

When I found myself crying in bed with him a week after Lev's funeral, I knew my first attempt to break it off with the iconoclast (after he had forgotten my birthday) had not, in fact, been successful. I began to search earnestly for something to distract me from my distraction. My casual dalliance with the iconoclast had become real and challenging and I found myself wanting something less; someone new, something other, but nothing more. The Blond Poet was (until he wasn't) a welcome diversion fueled, in part, by my drive to erase my desire for the iconoclast (whose siren song I was able to ignore in favor of the poet's for a brief while). Post-poet, I resisted the easy comfort of going back to Neverland. Instead, I took Joss home to my parents' house in Albany and walked the blizzard-paralyzed city. I walked my parents' neighborhood at night and watched the snow shine in the halos of streetlights, listened for the familiar squeaks and pops as my feet pressed the fresh-fallen powder into the texture of Styrofoam on the sidewalks under my boots.

On a late December afternoon, with the tinsel-bloat of Christmas still clinging to everything, I hovered outside a store in the mall while my mother and son shopped, busying myself with my phone as contemporary folks do. After weeks of nothing, my iconoclast had texted to tell me he wanted to take my photo. He'd discovered one last roll of Kodachrome—the iconic slide film, now discontinued—he'd need to shoot in the next twenty-four hours and send for processing before the last remaining lab in the country quit developing it at the turn of the new year. My heart swelled then broke a little. I was nowhere near, nor would I be for days. That we'd be star-crossed yet again was no bolt from the blue. It was just as well, really. No happy ending. The Rolling Stones' "Plundered My Soul" came out on an extended 2010 rerelease of *Exile on Main Street* and, as I played it on repeat and repeat and repeat as the worst year of my life ground me down to a powder, I was never so sure of anything as I was of the fact that this song was saving me and killing me all at once.

After the poet, there was a flirtation with a recent Brown graduate with Vampire Weekend sunglasses and a

Harvard scarf. He'd battled cancer and was about to enter medical school. He picked me a flower on his way to our first date. He wanted me to be impressed by these things. But I was not—my ex-husband graduated from Brown; my son died of cancer; I work in a hospital simply lousy with doctors. What else have you got, sir? He told me I made him nervous. And he gave up. Next, there was the PhD candidate from out of town with whom I thought I was developing a friendship founded in vocabulary and misfit snobbery. I thought him quite lovely on our afternoon at the museum, but he turned out, in truth, to be a gloomy misogynist who seemed to feel the principles of eminent domain were valid reasons why his tongue kept ending up in my mouth. After that debacle, I caved, went back to the well. I felt not the slightest bit distracted, but I kept on trying. In the spring, there was the lawyer who, on the strength of his looks and kisses, lasted the longest, but was not in fact well suited to me at all. My description of him prompted the iconoclast to ask: "Will you fall in love with him and stop coming to see me?" Obviously not. I'd arrived late to the poetry of Bob Dylan, and it hit me hard. Channeled through the pipes of nineteen-year-old Adele,

Dylan's words came at me like a laser. I scream-sang the verses of "Make You Feel My Love" in my car until I was hoarse and until the tears streamed down my face and until I knew them by heart backwards and forwards.

In my experience, stemming the tide of one's own brooding infatuation consists mainly of not continuing to sleep with the person who reduces you to a quivering mess. At this, I was a failure many times over. All manner of poet-shaped and other distractions served as evidence that perhaps my destiny, for a while at least, lay in this relationship that had begun as a distraction from the day-to-day slog of my crumbled and crumbling life and had come to be a security blanket I wasn't yet ready to give up. Perhaps it was not love or lust that would save me from my sadness. Perhaps I needed another outlet. I contemplated taking a group sewing class, but thought something more physical was probably in order. I looked into ballet. Once, I ran with my dog. But I got winded and felt like an asshole and promptly gave up. The nightlife was more my comfort zone, but what in the hell could I do there other than meet new boys to break my heart worse?

On one of his visits to town, I brought the PhD candidate to a comedy festival. I was friends with the guy who ran the thing so we had great seats and got to schmooze a bit and feel important. I had attended the same festival the year before and fallen head over heels in hero-worship with one of the comics. He was on the bill again this night and I was positively bursting at the seams to watch his new material. His set brought me to tears. Not tears of laughter, actual overflowing soul-deep tears. His work was insightful and reasoned and philosophical while simultaneously biting and hilarious and moving. I laughed too, of course, as hard as a person can laugh and still take in enough oxygen to stay conscious. Listening to this comedian kill made me as happy as I had been since Lev died. This. This was bliss.

I had been contemplating for a while the concept of trying stand-up comedy. Making light of the worst life had to offer was my one and only effective coping mechanism, and my tendency toward dazzle camouflage made me unafraid of putting on a show. At one point, in passing, I had bounced the idea off the iconoclast. Should I try stand-up? He reacted immediately. His eyes got wide and he told me I shouldn't. Changed the subject. I was so stunned, I didn't ask why. Regardless of the reason, I had held it in the back of my mind, felt maybe I needed to prove to myself that I was cut from the cloth of my idols. But could I do it? Could I own the room? Could I even get my shit together enough to do three minutes at an open mic? It would be a new kind of writing for me. It would take pathos and sincerity and boundless cynicism. And patience. I would be able to focus on very little else. And I would keep it from the iconoclast. I would do it for the first time in St. Louis, where I was headed for work in the spring. I had two months to plan and write. Fucking perfect. Done and done.

I had all of these thoughts and made the decision to venture into comedy in a fog of punch lines and endorphins during some wisp of a second between comedians. The PhD candidate and I went for a drink after the show and geeked out about the amazingness of what we'd just seen. At the end of the night he surprised me by trying to make out with me in a parking garage and we didn't see each other again. I didn't tell him about my plan to tell jokes onstage. I didn't tell anyone for a while. I was all jacked up with frustrated energy, which I poured into joke writing. And I was more than tenacious enough to get up on stage when I had the jokes to fill the time. I didn't care if I was awful (though somehow I knew I wouldn't be). I would be better eventually. And someday, I would kill.

SOLIPSISTS DO IT FOR THE FOLKS WATCHING AT HOME

In the winter after Lev's death, I operate on two speeds: suspended animation and blur. No in-between. There is the sound of gasping sobs inside my head, the TV droning in the next room. And there is the bombast of Out—an epic, bacchanalian roar. After four years as the lone cynic in a cellblock of the hopeful, I'm liberated. Everyone who knew Lev is still shackled, each now held underwater by their own grief, by its suddenness. I'm the opposite: I'm Houdini kicking free. It's three months since Lev's been gone, six months since I've left my house, two months since the clock started on my divorce. Valentine's Day— King Douchebag of made-up holidays—looms, bullying those loved and unloved alike into the purchase of cheap, pink boxes of bullshit. I struggle to feel some reverence for my past life; to conjure wistfulness, specifically, for the marriage I deserted. I can't. If the opposite of wistful is giddy, I'm that. I've proven myself inelegant at being single—mixing up my messages, never getting the tone quite right. Despite my ineptitude, I'm a dyed-in-the wool romantic. Always ready to fall in love again. I want to believe it's all still possible, that I haven't blown my allotment of chances at love and happiness.

I don't think I tried very hard to save my marriage. I stayed a long time after it was over. I think I wanted it to be okay. I know I worried a lot. Talked about it a lot. Anguished. Thought. Brooded. I wanted to feel better about things. But I don't recall doing very much. Taking real action. Things just kept falling apart harder and faster until there was rubble. My ex-husband swears he loved me. I don't know. Maybe, probably he did. What I can say with some degree of certainty is that he didn't know me very well, and he didn't love me my way, the way that I wanted. I wanted to be nurtured and understood. But in truth, I never loved him my way either. I wanted to

be loved with affection and abandon. I loved him pragmat-
ically and deliberately. I loved him in part because I was
convinced he could never break my heart. He was someone
upon whose calm fondness I could rely and return. In the
end, he became unpredictable; he became passionate about
things and people that were not me in a way we had never
really been passionate about each other. He poured himself
into a life to which I had no connection, and he followed a
dream I did not share. Without malice or intention, in the
end, he broke my heart. He says he loved me till the minute I told him there was no saving us. And then he tried
not to love me anymore. I was already long gone. For me,
everything changed long before the ultimate dissolution
of my marriage. We are in agreement on this. When I had
a miscarriage before Joss, the optimistic part of me went
dark and the loneliness became impenetrable—an electri-
fied fence; after that, there was no saving us.

After a torpedoed marriage, failed campaign to save my
son, retreat to my parents' empty condo—I've officially
botched my mission to be a functional grown-up human.
I'm a decommissioned ship as yet to find new life as a

floating museum. Suddenly, subtraction is all I can process. I never intended to have an only child, certainly not
by subtraction. But such is life. Subtract husband, responsibility, home. Subtract sad friends. Subtract fear. I wrestle
with this purge in my sessions with Old Fancy, my elegant therapist. Around this time, she and everyone else
weighing in tell me to give myself a break, that I've been
through a lot, I should live life and not worry so much.
Fuck them. All of them. I suspect I may be turning into
a terrible asshole, but I have subtracted giving-a-fuck.
Everything was awful and off-kilter, now maybe it can be
amazing, boundless, an orchard of perfect peaches, wind
in my sails and a waving sea all the way to the horizon.
There is no in-between.

The life I'd built over the preceding decade was one in
which I'd given a (very grave) fuck about what everyone
thought of me and of my choices. Now that Lev is gone, I
have a tragicomic amount of free time and little—save Joss,
whom I see only half the time—to anchor me. Fuck it, I'm
ready to stand with my half of Joss on the shore and give
the rest of it a Viking funeral, set it all on fire. Rise from

the ashes like an awkward past-her-prime phoenix. Take 2.
This time, the part of Me is played by pure, unfiltered Id.
I think not at all about how anything I might do will look
to the outside observer, how it might portray me to the
people watching. As a consequence, my plotline unfolds
as a slapstick sex-comedy. Watch if you must, I think, but
you're gonna get an eyeful. I fit my truest self into the
cracks, but I don't hide. Everyone is welcome to watch me
screw around and find my sea legs. For a while, I fall under
the spell of a couple. Him a laughing giant of a man whose
sleek body dwarfs mine and whose neck smells like home;
her an all-American beauty excellent at every sport, nur-
turing to pets and plants, but desiring no children of her
own. They are like foxes or wolves, gleeful pack predators
whose bite leads to long evenings of lazy consumption of
homemade pizzas and margaritas made with fresh limeade.
And sex. I get restless when they treat me like a snack. I
want to be sustenance. I move on. No in-between.

My old friends feel remote to me. It's harder for me to
experience their pain than my own. I can't help them. And
so, they can't help me. I make new friends. The friends on

whom I begin to rely are mostly younger than I am and childless. I'm a strange sort of celebrity among my new acquaintances, an item of gossip: "Oh my god, did you hear about what happened to her? Her son died. She's amazing. It's the worst. She's so strong . . ." Easy to simplify me this way, to boil me down to one-clause sentences that make me sound heroic. People seem to want to solve me or to bury me, to exalt me or count me out. It's less easy to just roll with me, to support me, to let me support them. Especially once they realize I have only two speeds—sprinting and broke-down. Many candidates quietly disappear. When I shed them like sandbags from a hot air balloon, I am lighter, leaner. Some of them don't last more than a conversation. Those who make the cut are all broken in some major way. Broken people are the only folks I can understand. People walking around intact, functional, hiding little to no darkness—these people frighten me. (This is not a new development. Even as a child, I exasperated my parents by bringing home the most bizarre feral-child creatures Public School No. 19 had to offer. I had a few ordinary, calm children as childhood friends, but they didn't endure.)

On Valentine's Day, I will host a white elephant party where every invited guest will bring a date they do not want. My new friends will come. I will hand out peacock feathers and drink French 75's and dance the Charleston. There will be a bearded gatecrasher and an unrequited infatuation between friends. There will not be new love. But there will be hope.

REMAINS AND RESTRAINTS

Lev's dad and I had originally planned to pick up our boy's ashes together, to soldier on in solidarity through another painful milestone, safety in numbers and all of that. But when the call came from the funeral home that the urn was ready to be picked up, the idea of playing family for the afternoon was untenable. Our previously strained relationship had degraded to the point we could barely tolerate being in the same room. Confident our tension would likely lead to a relationship meltdown in a totally inappropriate location, it was decided I would go and retrieve the urn solo. I scheduled the handoff appointment with the funeral director for a Friday at lunch in the hope that I could dash in and out with minimal interaction. Icon of crippling self-sufficiency that I am, I had of course declined all offers of accompaniment and support. I told myself it was because my shit was just that together, but there was a small part of me that wanted the option to blow the whole thing off out of sheer terror (and if I had someone meeting me there or driving me there, I would have to actually show up). Mostly, I was just unsure of what to expect from the situation and from myself once I was inside the belly of the beast. Best to go alone into the heart of darkness went my logic.

Turns out, returning to the funeral home for the urn weeks after the memorial was approximately like going back to the bar the morning after a night of hard drinking to retrieve your credit card. Where there had been ceremony and organ music and explosions of flowers in celebration of Lev's fantastic little life, now there was tatty carpeting and the awkward business of day-to-day funeral parlor operations: office clerks, fluorescent lighting, ringing phones. The funeral director (the same woman who had handled Lev's memorial—let's call her Norma) came out to the foyer to retrieve me and brought me into a small room with chintzy wallpaper and a large round table that dominated the space, filling it almost to the edges. Norma indicated that I should take a seat and she sat down next to me. I glanced around, but nowhere did I see the urn I had come to retrieve.

When Norma began talking about Lev and the memorial and how moved she had been by all of it, I got the message that her perceived bond with me was apparently strong on the heels of her admission of improv comedy aspirations weeks earlier. She wanted to share. It seemed like she wanted me to share too—I remember her asking me about my writing and about my job at the hospital, whether I had gone back to work yet. I suppose I must have answered her, but my half of our conversation has been redacted from my memory. Blank. What I do remember is the longer the exchange with Norma spun out, the less I understood the purpose of this meeting and the more I felt like I must have missed some key element of why we were there. My initial anxiety upgraded to mild panic as my confusion ratcheted up. I remember thinking: "Do we owe her money maybe? Is this her way of breaking the ice to shake me down for a check?"

Eventually, I know I started to cry. I remember the crying mostly because, ironically, there were no tissues in that room. (I came to the realization early on in the crying-a-hundred-times-a-day phase of my life that even in rooms where grief routinely comes to pass, there are never enough tissues. It's almost as if people willfully refuse to anticipate the messy moisture that comes with sadness. The bodily indignity with which grief presents us all is just too ugly, I suppose.) When it became clear that the dam had broken, Norma left the room and returned with a small packet of tissues for me. Not a whole box, mind you, but one of those tiny little cardboard packages like they have in hospitals. After a few uncomfortable minutes with me blowing my nose as the only soundtrack, Norma asked if I was ready to see the urn. "I think you'll be quite happy with it." She said. "It turned out beautifully." Already wrecked by the kookiness and oddly epic length of what I thought would be a mannered, brief interaction, I was resigned to go wherever this was headed. I nodded and followed Norma to the next, even weirder, location.

Unless and until you are responsible for retrieving the ashes of a cremated loved one, you would have no reason to know that the funeral home has a special little room for ceremonially displaying the urn. It's like a tiny chapel, not even big enough for a whole coffin. There are a couple of seats and a little pedestal for the urn. There are ferns and faux stained-glass windows and more tatty carpet. Basically, it's like an abbreviated churchy museum for displaying one box of dust. Lev's lacquered zebrawood box seemed extra out of place in the chapel setting. Not to mention we're Jews. Suffice it to say, the ash chapel took my sadness to a whole other plane of existential angst. Once in there, Norma and I commenced awkwardly shifting our weight and smiling at one another without making eye contact as it became clear that neither of us knew how long was long enough to wait in this moment. She starts to explain that the remains are additionally ensconced in a bag inside the box and shows me the mechanism for how they put the ashes in the urn. Oh, dear god. The length of time we were in that room couldn't have been more than five minutes, but in my mind, it was like Sartre's *No Exit*.

I wanted to grab the urn, stash it under my arm like a football, and run away. But I recognized that there must have been a process of some kind at work, something out of the funeral director playbook. Although said process was completely opaque to me, I was pretty sure my running blindly away from the scene was not the next thing on the agenda. Norma must have sensed my coiled energy ready to snatch my son's remains and bolt, because she grabbed the box off the pedestal and sheathed it in a velvet bag "so you don't get fingerprints on it." Then she led us out of the urn room, still clutching the package. I loped along behind her, baffled, as we made our way toward the front door. She paused in the foyer to ask me where I'd parked and whether I wanted to bring the car around. Keep in mind, it's not raining, the parking lot is small, and the parcel in question is a box weighing maybe three pounds. I have no idea where she's going with this, but I humor her because it's clear she has a plan. So I go and get the car and pull it under the carport and Norma comes out to meet me, cradling the urn. I keep thinking: OK, this is it. She's definitely going to hand me the urn now. Any minute now. But she stands there stone-faced, waiting. So,

I fumble with the locks to the back door, thinking she'll place the box on the seat and I can peel out in a puff of tire smoke. Instead, Norma opens the front passenger door, and begins to *strap Lev's urn into the front passenger seat with the seat belt* as I look on in horror. And then, she looks me in the face with total beatific sincerity, tilts her head to the side like she's got some emotion welling up and says, without irony, "Well, I guess this is the only time he'll get to ride in the front seat . . ." and trails off.

I broke Norma's gaze. Blinked. Clicked my own seat belt into the latch. And as I finally turned the key in the ignition, the box of Lev riding shotgun beside me, I resisted the urge to peel out, drove away in an orderly fashion. When I got back to my parents' sterile condo, I sat in the car for a few minutes to let it all wash over me. I cried some. And then I started to giggle. And the laughter kept coming more and harder, culminating as I unstrapped the seat belt from the urn to walk my son's remains into a house where he never lived, one of the single oddest moments of my life up to that point. I thought to myself: *That all actually happened.*

It totally happened and it kept on happening. And it was both soul raping and hilarious. You can't make this stuff up. And, why would you? It's all right there. Those moments where humor is so crushingly deadpan and black that you are compelled to break the fourth wall of your sadness and fucking melt into the kind of convulsive laughter that reroutes your day—those are the moments that saved me. Instead of going back to work that afternoon, I drove downtown, got a really expensive manicure and sat in the spa until dusk. It was kind of glorious.

ALL EXITS LOOK THE SAME

Lev's death was followed by literal and figurative winter, so cold it hurt to breathe. I existed in a state of exhausted incurable chill. Deadened. The dreams I had of Lev in the season following his death were almost universally nightmares. Sometimes he was the walking dead, a corpse but somehow still dying. In the dreams I would hold him close, afraid I'd break his fragile decomposing body but unable to let him go. In these moments, he would sometimes speak to me, but I could never hear his tiny voice. Sometimes it was all I could do to meet his gaze because when he looked back at me, it was with judgment for the way in which I'd dreamed him. His caregivers would often appear in these dreams, asking about Lev's medicines, about how to tend to him now that he was back, as if his death had been greatly exaggerated and it was now time to get back to our quotidian reality. I seemed always to be the only one who understood that Lev was still dead; that there had been no miracle. And in these dreams, I always know he'll be gone in an instant. As they're happening, I know he's not there at all. I wake up devastated. I've not rested. I'm haunted.

During the winter, the void left by the subtraction from my life of one and a half children and a husband was unquantifiable. I couldn't see its edges; my vessel had come unmoored. Impatient to feel functional, instead I felt razed. For strength, I talked to Lev. I told my littlest son how much I miss him every second. How lost I am at any given moment. And I admitted aloud and that nothing will ever be quite okay. I touched his urn. I held his toys. I stood in the middle of the room and wept. I kept a tiny heart-shaped pendant full of his ashes on a long chain, sometimes tucked into my clothes, sometimes sparkling on the outside (I've rubbed it between my fingers so much that its texture has changed). For a time, I experienced shooting pains in my arms. Holding a ghost is cold comfort.

My support system had roared to life for Lev's funeral. Family and friends came to Texas from what seemed like other planets. Some sent envoys. A few of my in-town friends deliberately stayed away. They couldn't help, either because they didn't know how or because they knew there was no role for them. Most of my in-town friends were parents of sick children or people who worked at the hospital or parents of Joss's friends. They were there in the morass with me, but most had boundaries to keep. And I had nothing to offer anyone except wide-eyed fog. Once the dust settled, I was mostly alone. I kept time with virtual strangers. I craved closeness and nearness in my friendships, but the idea of forging new bonds was overwhelming. So much had been laid to waste in the years that Lev was dying. Storied relationships with history and weight were trampled, set afire and burned to ashes, or froze during the winter following. Friendships with really good private jokes and entire albums of photos on Facebook were lost and left for dead.

One night I came home to the empty condo to find a tall thin box held together with packing tape and propped against the front door. Standing in the dark, I could read the return address written in a neat hand in black magic marker. It was from an old friend and his wife who hadn't been able to make it to Lev's memorial, but whom I'd talked to almost every day. When I opened the box, inside it were ninety-nine origami paper cranes. The birds overflowed the edges like they were alive, falling like fledglings. I read the card nestled in the center of the flock. And then I melted into a puddle. They folded a hundred birds for me and for Joss as a symbol of all of the things you want to put into words but you just can't because it's all too gigantic and symbolic and it sounds tinny when you try and speak about it. They sent ninety-nine of them. The hundredth crane they kept for their unborn baby's room, as a reminder of all of that huge precious stuff. Stuff I needed to remember. Of which I'd needed to be reminded. My sad brain could be tricky about forgetting all that I still had.

My frozen personality, in these months, could be mistaken, at first glance, for placid or spacey or sycophantic, even. I had a vast network of acquaintances and I went where they told me to go. I met them in those places for drinks and dinners. I watched their favorite films and I read the books they recommended. I slept with their friends. As I started to wake up and realize I was no longer content to trip along behind whoever had invited me wherever, I had more time than I knew what to do with. The dwellers in the cracks of my life were no longer sufficient to fill these endless hours. While I figured out how to be something resembling myself again or maybe for the first time, I made playlist after playlist and put them on the internet like messages in a bottle. I started a blog. I joined an online dating site. I did everything I thought I was too good for—to prove to myself that I could be humbled. Or perhaps "tamed" is a better word. Or maybe broken, like a horse. The question of how to make new friends at thirty-six—how to be open to it, even—began to obsess me. Commence awkward relationship-building adolescent phase—brutal, but totally necessary.

I could not have imagined the spectacular failures of some of the relationships I began. For a person who lives as deeply inside their head as I do, it's funny to me that no amount of thinking could have predicted the fallout and the key takeaways from these implosions, all of which I carefully reported to my faraway friends for guidance and help in processing the way forward. One woman whom I met shortly after Lev died made a convincing case for friendship: friends in common, similar interests, large vocabularies, similar senses of humor. The next few times we met, she introduced me to other people to whom she'd recounted the romantic dimensions of my loss, my whole story. I wasn't sure what to make of it. It felt rushed to me, too intense. Almost like she was enamored of the things about me that she knew (and in getting caught up, she was missing the degree to which these were events I had been a part of, not qualities I possessed). In my head, I thought maybe this was just how new friendships felt? That the longer we knew one another, the more the comfort level would increase. Instead, things unraveled spectacularly and she would eventually decide I was awful—the worst. She sat me down and flat-out told me she felt disillusioned.

There were very real reasons why our friendship wouldn't have worked. Some of them were mistakes I made, errors in judgment, times I acted like an asshole. But in the end, this almost-friend told me she had come to the conclusion she'd misjudged me as a person; that I was not the sort she wanted to know. There was no recovering. The way I saw it, the miserable (but somehow noble) grief-stricken version of me was more palatable to her (and maybe to a lot of people) than the woman I aimed to get back to being. As compelling and sad as my story might be, the person who had lived through it was (is) still way under construction. Surviving a series of terrible life events didn't make me beatific. It didn't erase my flaws. I was and am sad and strong, but still just me. Despite the perspective that came with fighting valiantly and losing Lev, I can be as self-involved and bitchy as anyone I know. If you were hoping to meet a paean to selflessness, someone gracious and uncynical—well, I'd like that for you too. Sadly I'm not that someone. I am over-wordy and awkward. I can be the worst kind of crashing introvert and miss the signals that I've gone too far. I mostly mean well. But I'm not for everyone.

To rally from this confusing setback, I would need reinforcements: people who got what they were signing up for in knowing me, forgiving folk who understood the ugliness of my personality reconstruction. At the very least, I needed people who would live and let live, who I could go out with to big fun parties, who would share a cab home with me from the bars and not hold me to unrealistic expectations (or preferably any expectations). I knew this would not be the last mess I'd get into, but I resolved to try for better. And sure enough, in the spring, dormant acquaintances blossomed into shade trees of iron. I could not have imagined how the people who were already in my life as bit players or those I held at arm's length would come to be so important to me. How much I would want to know them better and protect them and vice versa. I added them to my phone contacts and followed them on social networks. I drank their shots and their wine. I listened to their advice. I sought their approval. I lay in bed with them and laughed. Cried. Comforted them. I gave them what I had. I took what they offered. In short, I made friends.

The sum total of spring amounted to something like banging out the first draft of a new life: get it all down, full of mess. Edit later. In an effort to outfox the black hole nesting in my ribcage, I'd come out of the gate hard, plowing through my first six post-Lev months like a bull in a china shop—aware but unable or unwilling to slow down or pause for reflection. I got basically nothing right but it didn't exactly matter. Keep moving. Like a shark. Because no one tells the shark, "You're doing it wrong."

POOR RELATIONS

It's 9 p.m. I'm in St. Louis, sitting at a table with three nurses in an Irish pub called O'Malley's. As I nurse my first vodka tonic (by no means my last) of the night, I'm scanning the place for a guy who looks like his name could be Max. Max has The List. You sign up with Max. There are a couple of regular looking patrons and a bartender who has already assured me he's not Max. It's empty here. Every time the door opens, my breath catches. I'm wondering, am I even in the right place?

It's the first Monday in May, 2011. Osama Bin Laden is dead. St. Louis is recovering from being slammed by a tornado ten days earlier. When we'd taxied in from landing at the airport on Sunday, we could see the windows

of the airport still boarded up from the storm. It's cold
for spring in St. Louis, hovering around 50 degrees and
raining all day—for weeks, actually. I'm here for work, for
a health care conference, surrounded by nurses and doctors talking about serious things. In the morning, while
the light was still dim, I'd stumbled bleary-eyed into the
grand ballroom of our hotel to lead my team through the
first of three long, dry days of learning.

I've also come to St. Louis to grab a certain brass ring
for myself. Tonight. For six weeks, I've been preparing
for this trip. The night we arrived in town, I'd quietly
searched the internet for this place or for someplace like
this—someplace my speed. O'Malley's is starting to fill
up with scruffy twentysomethings carrying notebooks.
I'm definitely in the right place. As I get up for a drink
and take a lap around the room, I see I'm easily ten to fifteen years older than nearly everyone here. The energy in
the bar is getting more intense, but no one is gravitating
toward any one dude yet. These kids with their notebooks
seem to know. Max has not yet arrived on the scene with
the list. It's 10 p.m.

A few minutes later, the door of the bar opens and the energy in the room shifts. This is him. Max. He waves to his friends and sets up across the room with a notepad and a pen. The notebook kids surge across the room to sign up for the comedy open mic—the reason we're all here. I feel for a second like I'm going to pass out; my head gets real swimmy. I pound the vodka in front of me and I'm warm and slightly less panicked. I get up and walk over to join the throng assembled in front of Max. I get my name in and I'm number nine on the list. The List. Number nine. I will be ninth to tell my jokes. Well okay then.

Rewind. 10 a.m. Shortly after the morning conference session begins, my cell phone buzzes. When I step outside of the hotel ballroom to take the call, I can see my breath. I huddle under an eave of the building to escape getting stabbed by needles of cold drizzle. The call is from my ex-husband. There's a problem he needs me to help solve and I can't do it because I'm in St. Louis. It gets ugly quickly. The whole conversation is exhausting and results in me screaming at him that I will call my dad and my dad will have him arrested—a threat upon which I have no intention of following through, but for some reason I think is important to make at the time. I put my head in my hands and cry in the rain before I go back in to the conference. I feel crazy and backed against the wall. I have to step outside several more times to put this situation closer to right. In a lighter moment, I make the mistake of telling him I might do stand-up for the first time later that night. He tells me the concept mortifies him. I'm crestfallen. I consider abandoning my comedy ambitions for the evening.

In the first afternoon breakout session from the larger conference, each of the participants is asked to go around the table and tell our story and—as usual—I bring the room to a screeching halt with mine. I realize in that moment, if I let the difficult reality of my history—or of my day-to-day life—derail my sense of humor, the terrorists (or in this case, the jerks) win. I decide to go through with the open mic no matter what shit show this day has in store for me. There's always a brass ring. Sometimes it's unattainable—like finding a cure for cancer or bailing a sinking ship of a marriage. And sometimes it's just stepping on the stage and telling a fucking joke. The trip, for me, is now about getting on stage at O'Malley's Irish Pub and getting laughs.

———•———

As a small kid, I remember having a crush on Steve Martin (that never stopped, actually). In high school, I wooed boys with my exhaustive repertoire of cribbed stand-up comedy routines. In college, we made a ritual of saving our money and taking the train downtown to see Emo Phillips and Judy Tenuta. I don't think it's putting too fine a point on it to say that I had been grooming myself my whole life to get onstage and tell jokes. If not to build a career out of it, then to be able to understand from the inside how complex and interesting and punishing a pursuit comedy—ironically—is at its heart. I wanted to know better that which I loved.

In truth, I wasn't coming to comedy as a total outsider. And that may have hurt me more than helped. Austin, where I live, is a town densely packed with humorists of all stripes. One of my oldest and dearest friends—I call him the overlord—curates the granddaddy of our city's many comedy festivals. I'd seen countless shows, been moved to tears, and met my idols through him. The flipside of that kind of access was feeling out of my element and exposed when it came to the idea of trying my hand at stand-up. I was afraid that my sense of my own viability as a performer had become inflated during the time I'd been preparing to come out of the comedy closet, watching so many talented people swimming in the pool. I wondered if perhaps I was sort of talentless. Not something I—or anyone—could know, though, without trying out my material and letting the audience decide.

Before I left for St. Louis, I contemplated entering a local stand-up contest in Austin. I had thus far played my desire to tell jokes on stage pretty close to the vest, and when I mentioned to the overlord I was thinking of competing, his reaction was first and foremost protective. He recommended against it with a firmly furrowed brow. And though he'd helped me workshop jokes and been supportive of my humorous predilections, he wasn't sure any of this was a good idea. Not sure I should do it at all. I wasn't sure enough, myself, to argue otherwise. I decided, for this reason, I couldn't start out in Austin. I would second-guess myself right out of ever trying. This is roughly how I ended up in the ladies' room of a Landry's seafood restaurant in St. Louis, MO, staring at a pair of underwires from a bra on the floor of the bathroom stall and rewriting my jokes on the way to the show.

———

As the comedians on the list before me go up one by one and do their sets, I think about the overlord and the other people who—out of protectiveness, fear, or just plain not getting it—have told me I should not do this. I wish I could pack this room with them, but the point of doing these jokes in St. Louis is that it's not Austin. Because just in case I fall on my face, fuck if I'm going to fall on my face at home. I drink another two vodkas really fast. The guy before me does seven minutes about masturbating with two dicks. Kill me. During his set, two other people move their slots on the list so as not to follow him. When he's done, I take the mic, breathe, and step onstage . . .

"Ladies and gentlemen, I'm here to tell you: I have become my poor relations. You know the ones—the ones who are proud that they live in a triple-wide? Yeah, you know. This morning I threatened to call the cops on my ex for breaking down the door of my apartment after his spare tire was stolen off the front lawn of my ex-house. I was making a go of being classy for a while. But that's over. Tonight, I ate at a Landry's and was surprised to find a pair of underwires from a bra on the floor of the bathroom. I know, right? In such a fancy place . . . you know who thinks Landry's is a fancy place? Say it with me: Poor relations . . .

"The city where I live has been absolutely overrun by hipsters. But it's gotten to the point where I'm not sure they notice they've lost the element of rebellion and are dressing like my dad in the 1960s—like, nicely tailored pants and cardigans and black-framed glasses? It's like watching bored Buddy Holly eat trailer food and listen to DJ music . . .

"And so, I said to myself, either he thinks escorts are relationship coaches, or he thinks relationship coaches are escorts. But either way, he paid for the happy ending. Thanks, everyone. You've been great. Goodnight . . ."

My set goes passably well. A few bobbles, a few laughs. Not perfect, but not at all a failure. Afterward, milling about outside the bar with the other comics, a girl quotes one of my jokes back to me—the one about the cardigan. Holy fuck. I text the overlord from the cab on the way home and tell him what I've done. He's proud of me. I am so very proud of me too.

STATISTICALLY SIGNIFICANT

The first time I signed up, it was because I wanted to know what the fuss was about. I answered hundreds of questions and uploaded flattering photos. Crafted a witty bio, listed my favorite things in the categories of music and films and books and foods. I made my profile on the dating site and I promised myself I'd give it a week. Technically, I lasted five days.

My husband and I had opened up our relationship during the thick of the worst of Lev's cancer treatment. We wanted to keep living together and to stay married as long as we could stand one another even if it meant quietly screwing around. Don't ask, don't tell, we said. How modern of us. Turns out, we both unwittingly joined the same online dating site. Because of course we did. The site immediately pegged us as a 98 percent match (exhausting!) and my husband messaged me within hours of my putting up a profile. I blocked him. In all fairness, I blocked a lot of people. In my recollection, my first stab at online dating was a nonstop barrage of attention from men who felt they knew me from a few photos and my carefully chosen words. The tone of blithe familiarity from these strangers was the same kind of unpleasant as a bug flying into your mouth while you're walking. No self-awareness. No grasp of manners or self-deprecation or ice-breaking. I was too good for this nonsense. I had too much dignity. Not to mention, the prospect of meeting new people, of having to remember which things about my life I pretended to love and which parts I was allowed to openly hate, threatened to expose the sham of my existence quite handily. I couldn't seem to get to the humble place or the shameless place. Just couldn't get there.

Though I very much wanted to be ready, it was clear to me that I was nowhere near prepared to date; to explain to these probably perfectly nice men—who simply wanted

to have dinner with a pretty girl and maybe feel her up—
that I was separated from my husband, but we were still
living together because our child was dying. After five
days of feeling intense pressure to commit to an actual
date with any number of strangers who seemed sort of
okay, I shut down my profile and went back to hiding on
the iconoclast's couch. In the wee small hours, I'd talk
to him for hours about everything that scared me. He'd
talk me down and then we'd screw till I was calm and
calm and calm. At the end of my world, he was my fallout
shelter.

I am way more attractive at thirty-six than I was as a
teenager or in my twenties. The angles of my face have
gotten sharper and the curves of my body have grown
softer. I am dotted with a map of tattoos, mile markers
of the things that have shaped me. My deeply ingrained
awkwardness is well mitigated by sexual confidence. I am
certain that despite the near total ruin of my life, this is
the best I've ever been. Humility, however, is not a quality I would ascribe to myself. I am vain and a know-it-all,
dyed-in-the-wool.

The second time I ventured into the online dating pool, it was because I wanted to be humble. I had messed things up with (or fled from) all of the men I loved, the ones who'd loved me, and all of the men my friends had introduced me to. I was sick to death with myself and with the optimism of maybe-this-time. I had proven whatever I had to prove (mostly I proved I was excellent at hiding behind an armor of snark and disdain). Now I wanted to be quiet and docile and do things like everyone else. I needed the comfort of an algorithm, some kind of statistical formula that made it at least likely that I might jibe with some man in particular. I wanted to make statistical sense of it all.

Online dating is a unifying, homogenizing experience. It's one of those things that, no matter how rich or posh or cool you are, you can't send a minion to do it for you. You have to show up and be counted. It's like the DMV. You are just like every other sad, broken socially awkward person you judge as you're scrolling through your reject pile. And odds are, you're in someone else's reject pile. You've taken the time to make a profile on an online dating site and that makes you—in essence—just like the fat guy in the tank top and neon orange sunglasses holding a fish, a deer, or another animal he had just killed. You're on par with the guy in military fatigues who may or may not have shot his profile photo at Abu Ghraib. You hope, just like they hope, to be someone's perfect match. Or maybe you think: it can't hurt. And maybe, probably, it can't. You belong there with everyone else simply because you made the choice to show up and be counted.

In version 2.0 of my online dating adventure, I made dates. Lots and lots of dates. I strategically set them up sometimes two per night to meet as many people as possible. To be open; to really do it. I met some lovely folks and some less lovely. Consider these, a selection of guys-I-went-out-with-once, for your reading pleasure:

There was the rockabilly ringer for Steve Buscemi, who I met up with once at 1 a.m. for one drink. Tattooed from neck to fingers, he was a touring musician. He teared up when I told him about Lev. We made out for a minute by the car. Sweet, but not for me.

He was followed by the guy who wrote freelance math problems and insisted intelligence was not a quality he valued in other people. He was in a competitive karaoke troupe and took the bus because his Mercedes was rusting out on his front lawn. We had lunch. I dropped him off afterward. We had no chemistry.

I ate a Cobb salad on my date with the former Mormon. He and I traded mixtapes (I still listen to his). I was impatient with his niceness which bordered on pandering. He was tortured about his ex-wife. Too soon.

The man who wore clogs to our date was a builder in his late forties, depressed that his wife had left him after he'd constructed her dream house from scratch. He told me he'd biked through the sub-Saharan region in his youth and it seemed to him that every woman in Africa has a dead baby. He tried to kiss me.

The one I called Bright Eyes was cagey. We met up once in the evening to eat and drink and make out (and once more in the afternoon because good chemistry bears revisiting).

We were pretty much done after that. Though I proceeded to run into him no less than ten times around town. With my kid. With my friends. With other dates.

The only man I dated more than twice showed up on my page a few weeks into my odyssey of online dating—an attorney who rode BMX bikes and built bike trails for fun; good looking, clean-cut but rough around the edges. We traded a few emails. He was a decent writer, not super witty, but he kept up. I was drawn in. At the end of our first date, he kissed me goodnight and there was a spark. Right there is where I got mind-fucked by good on paper. Because with online dating, you're invested before you ever even meet the person. You've invested time poring over their photos and texting back and forth and telling all of your friends about how perfectly their music taste matches yours. And if you're me, once you meet the first halfway decent person in a month of trying and he gives you one good kiss, you give that person six too many chances.

Good-on-Paper and I alternated planning dates. We saw music, ate great meals, and attended culturally significant events in museum lobbies. After our third date, I found out that—in addition to being good on paper—he was also good in the sack. Somehow, though, on every one of our dates, even the ones I'd planned, I was maddeningly bored. He talked about nothing but hating his job and BMX and when I tried to lighten things up, it always seemed to me that he didn't quite get my jokes. He would say: "Ha! That's funny." But not laugh? It seems Mr. Good-on-Paper was a good time black hole. So. The world-class burlesque show bored me to tears. The reading of my favorite author (to which Good-on-Paper showed up on his motorcycle) was a total snoozefest. I just kept thinking it's GOT to be ME. He's a lawyer. He rides BMX bikes and does tricks! He doesn't have a roommate! Or an ex-wife! He's so rare. Like a unicorn. I tried to make it work for two months.

Eventually, he asked me to help him redecorate his place. And I realized that he wanted to see more of me than I wanted to see of him. It seemed like a fitting time for an exit. I broke up with Good-on-Paper without tears or even sadness. But I was discouraged. He was the only one out of all of my many dates who even threatened to have any

potential whatsoever. We tried to have a drink after we
stopped seeing each other, but it was a (boring) mistake.
At the end, he tried to get me to come home with him. I
had an early flight out of town in the morning and I was
in no mood to relive the magic of rolling around with the
past. I went home happily alone and took a much-needed
break from treading water in the online dating pool.

A week after my comedy debut in St. Louis, I'm on vacation
in Los Angeles, visiting the offspring of my friends. (Like
salmon, all of my friends spawned at the same time and
during that five-day sojourn in L.A., I visited something
like eight babies of people I knew—all under eighteen
months old.) I'm holed up in my friend's rambling Vic-
torian house in Echo Park getting ready for dinner when
a particularly clever message comes in via my phone's
online dating app.

I look up this clever fellow's profile. His writing is wry
and spare. He's heartthrob handsome in his photo—jacket

and tie, sandy brown curls, downcast blue eyes—but with the saddest face. It breaks my heart a little. I don't message him back right away, but I do eventually. And we meet. He's drier than dry. Funny. Razor-sharp. He's cute and floppy haired and sullen like the boys in the posters on my high school bedroom walls. And his face in person—as on his profile—is sad and so worried. But in the rare moments when he smiles, his face opens like windows. It takes my words away. I see him again.

If the iconoclast was my fallout shelter, this melancholy boy who found me on the internet was waiting for me, hand extended, when it was safe to come outside.

NO MAS

There exists, in the annals of psychology, the concept of Replacement Child Syndrome. Put simply, Replacement Child Syndrome comes to pass when, after losing a child, a woman becomes pregnant again in an effort to start over, to erase the loss, to fold the potential of the dead child into a new vessel. Children conceived after the death of a sibling often fill a specific role in their parents' coping schema, helping to sop up the grief and redirect sadness, sometimes—according to the literature—with mixed-to-negative effects on the children themselves. A cursory Google search shows significant writing on the subject—both academic and anecdotal—by clinicians as well by mothers and grown "replacement children." On her blog *The Forgotten Grief,* Elizabeth Kirkley Best described

". . . the observation of hundreds of researchers and counselors who have noted for 50 years the existence of what has been termed the 'replacement child syndrome', a phenomenon in which many feelings about the 'ideal' child that died are overlaid on the feelings regarding the next child who survives. Many historical examples have been noted of pathological examples in which the 'new' child cannot live up to the expectations of what the previous child would have been like." Intriguingly a number of famously successful creative minds—John Coltrane, Peter Sellars, Vincent van Gogh, and Sigmund Freud among them—were born subsequent to the death of a sibling and are generally thought to have been "replacement children" in the definitional sense.

During the chaotic spring after Lev died, I received an unexpected email. It was from the girlfriend to whom I had been closest as a teenager, and with whom I'd grown frustratingly distant in recent years. As young women who had only brothers, we fancied ourselves as sisters—sharing everything, fighting with, consoling, and protecting one another. When she'd spent the summer after our freshman year in college in Paris, we'd kept journals so we could trade them upon her return, so we'd not miss out on a moment of each other's day-to-day lives. As adults, we lived in opposite corners of the country and rarely saw one another, especially after our children were born. In the months after Lev's death, we'd grown even farther apart.

Shortly before Christmas, she'd told me she was twenty-five weeks pregnant with her second child. She had been in her second trimester when she'd heard the news that Lev had died. She'd been reluctant to tell me about her pregnancy, even as Lev was still living, because she knew he wasn't doing well and she didn't want to assault me with her happy news. She'd frankly told me she wasn't sure I would be okay with hearing about her pregnancy and so she'd kept it to herself. In my estimation, her reticence about her good fortune correlated directly with how poorly she understood me. If she could be so misguided as to not comprehend that, not only could I handle the happiness of those closest to me—in fact, I thrived on it, that it damn well kept me going—well, maybe she didn't know me at all. At the time, I couldn't get past it. I let our relationship founder as I retreated into my winter cocoon of long nights and short days and general blackness of heart.

On a bright-eyed March morning, I opened an email from this woman with cautious optimism, thinking she was set to give birth in the next few weeks, wondering how she was doing, hoping we could perhaps mend fences. Instead of good tidings, though, there was unfathomable sadness, described matter-of-factly over the internet: three weeks earlier, after weeks of nesting, getting their house ready, my friend had stopped feeling the baby move inside her. She had gone to her doctor and to the hospital for tests. They could detect no heartbeat. The baby, it was determined, had died. They induced labor thirty-six weeks into her pregnancy. My friend gave birth to a stillborn son, whom she and her husband held and named Henry. Spontaneous fetal death, they called it. Autopsy showed no reason, gave no comfort. Since it happened, my friend had been hiding in quiet, taking long walks. She couldn't find words to speak about it. She wondered if I had any insight into talking with others about Henry, helping them to feel better. For my friend and her second child,

I wept my eyes dry and sobbed my throat raw. When she and I finally spoke, I told her that I was certain there were no words that could help; no words she could speak that would make others feel better, not yet anyway. She should rest in the quiet if it brought her comfort. And I would be there in the quiet with her if she wanted. We were sisters once more, bound by unimaginable loss.

By summer, my friend and her husband were working at getting pregnant again. I admired their resolve, their optimism. In my work at the hospital, I had seen other families do exactly this thing. I had met more than a few babies conceived as their older sibling was dying of a terminal illness, some born within days of the older child's death. Replacement Child Syndrome didn't seem to apply here, though perhaps I just didn't see or understand it yet. There was a peace about these families, a solidness that seemed to spring from new hope in the form of a fresh life. I wished to want this. But I did not. I do not.

There was a time, though, in the months before Lev died, when I was consumed with the desire to have another baby. At the frenzied end of my life as Lev's mother, I felt an almost pathological urge to get pregnant, to tamp out the coming gloom, to distract myself from the definite sadness with a chaotic new beginning. The idea of having another child with my three-year-old slowly dying, my marriage in shambles, was in all ways unsound. My logical mind frowned upon it. But my instinct, my very guts wanted to replace a dying child with a chance at a full life: one for one. In the fantasy, this imaginary baby with whom I would become pregnant would be a girl. Oh, how I wanted a baby girl. The endless possibilities of pink things with bows and all sorts of nothing-like-before felt like the answer to every question. Hormones and grief stage-whispered into my mind's ear a Moebius loop of coercion. My body—my empty womb—conspired to outsmart my mind at every turn. I fortified my birth control regimen, buttressing my ladyparts against all possible invaders. It was to be an epic battle, but one I would win.

As poetic as nature can be, allowing us to make a new baby at will when one is lost, no child in the history of the universe has ever solved its parents' problems by being born.

Infants are grueling. They're impossibly fragile and needy and irrational and keep to no schedule, listen to no reason. And yet, they are enrapturing, borderline-magical in their ability to make one feel useful, to give purpose and meaning: a reason for being. And we imbue our offspring additionally with meaning and promise and potential to make us more than we are. That existential drive is how Lev came into being in the first place. My husband and I were in a tense standoff about the matter of our as yet theoretical second child. He wanted another baby immediately upon meeting the first baby, our perfect and delightful Joss. Enthralled with the wonder of his spawn, he fervently wanted another, and within scant weeks of Joss's birth, he wanted to try again. I was frankly terrified of ruining the first one, let alone ready for another. I wanted to wait, so our children would be—somewhat arbitrarily—three years apart. Mostly I was stalling.

In one of the great paradoxes of humanity, a person is only truly capable of knowing whether they'd be a good parent once they're thrust irreversibly into the role. When Joss was born, I felt the pressure to excel at parenting, but never the confidence that I was qualified for the job. Anxiety about my parenting chops notwithstanding, I also felt the pressure to have another baby; pressure not just from my husband and parents, but also from myself. I should follow through with what I'd always wanted, with the plan we'd made. I resisted for a while, put a moratorium on even talking about another baby until I could get my head around the concept. I relented, eventually, because I was weak with lack of sleep and suggestible to my husband's excitement. And so I got pregnant on the evening of my thirty-second birthday. Our children would be two years apart. I supposed if nothing else, this baby would solve the problem of my resisting having more children. As it happened, Lev didn't solve any problems with his birth; instead his birth unleashed the fire of every anxiety and fear a parent could have. And then drowned the fire in a flood of nightmarish grief. And Joss became an only child. Again.

As I picked through the rubble of my life after Lev's death, looking for scraps to save, I realized with some certainty that I did not want to get married again or have more children. I didn't view the realization as a deficiency or based in fear. I wasn't resistant to finding love again. In the event that I found someone with whom I wanted to spend the rest of my life, I favored the idea of living in the moment, not locking down a future. Marriage I'd done once through. It didn't work out. Once was enough. It felt something like relief to admit to myself that maybe I had never been wired for forever in the first place. And having more children was simply not something I wanted or needed or felt I could handle. In Joss, I had all I needed in the way of species-propagation. And Lev will be with me for the rest of my days, looking out at me from photos, dancing for me in video clips shot in my old living room to music I loved in 2009. It was enough to have had two children, even if only briefly.

My friends, who were for the most part just venturing out into the world of marriage and family as I was exiting, almost universally responded with skepticism to my resolve not to do it all again. They thought it must be some outside influence that led me away from the path I'd always been on. And in a small way, they were right. It was the men I dated who made me examine my thoughts on the subject of marriage and family. The men who saw fit to date the broken hull of me in the months following Lev's death were understandably curious about my thoughts on starting over. Each seemed varying degrees of disappointed when I said I was not at all interested in marrying them (or anyone) and/or having their babies. One doesn't think of babies and wedding cakes dancing in the eyes of bachelors of any age. Certainly, the desire to nest and reproduce doesn't radiate from the average thirtysomething male. But even the weakly reflected drive of these men to settle down made me realize I wanted the opposite. It occurred to me—and I said it aloud to more than one of them: to the Blond Poet, to Good-on-Paper—these men didn't need to date me, a thirty-six-year-old divorcee with a kid and a mountain of grief. They needed to find young, fresh twenty-something girls with their whole lives ahead of them. They needed Daisy Buchanan in *The Great Gatsby*. I was the one Daisy hit with Gatsby's car.

To be fair, I guess it wasn't that I wanted the opposite of marriage and children so much as I wanted no part of milestones or future planning or next steps. I wanted to live here and now. Children and marriage had proven hard, mean, terrifying. I had some peace, some control now. My world was small; my son was only. This was it for me. This was enough.

MUSEUM OF SORROWS

I feel sometimes like I'm asleep, like I'm sleepwalking through everything. Like I will only remember the months after my son's death in the patchy, vaguely creepy, déjà-vu way in which one remembers a dream. This is how I remember the time when I let go of my house.

The sale of the house was meant to be healing. I imagined it as a shedding of the vestiges of my life that had gone so wrong. A cleansing breath. In the end, it felt like drinking poison. Though I had been the one to leave, my resentment at failing at marriage and family, my sadness at losing the people and things I'd loved, was no less potent. I hadn't lived there in months and could barely bring myself to cross the threshold into this place I'd labored so hard to make a home. I still loved it, of course. My estranged husband and I had agreed to sell the house before finalizing our divorce. We agreed this because our house was haunted. In the end, though, selling the place, letting it go, solved nothing. I brought the sadness with me. The ghosts were everywhere.

When my marriage fell apart, I decided to leave our house and decamp to an apartment my parents owned. It was a financial decision; neither my husband nor I had any money to spare and it seemed kinder to do it this way. The new place had no memories. I hated it there. It was the place where I landed when I ran away from home. I tried to decorate, to make it feel warm there. But I pined for my house, for the house where my children's sandbox lived and my favorite chair, a place where I had last been happy and hopeful, pregnant with Joss, drinking hibiscus tea and buying art for the children's nursery. Most painfully, I pined for Lev's house. I felt far away from Lev's life in this sterile, tiny apartment, miles from all of his things and from the place where he danced in videos to the music of 2009 and watched Elmo in our bed.

My husband hated living in the house where we had been a family, where everything went wrong. He wanted nothing more than to be rid of it, called it the Museum of Sorrows. Without my constant screaming fits of nagging, my husband let the house decay around him. He and Joss lived like squatters among piles of toys and books and clean laundry left unfolded. It broke my heart to go home. Before we put the house on the market, my husband undertook every renovation we never did while we lived there: patched all of the cracks in the walls, repainted all the rooms, landscaped the backyard. It made my heart ache to see the place beautiful again. Once it was ship-shape, I staged it for sale. I hung new paintings, bought accessories and candles and throw pillows and plants. I made it perfect. And it sold quickly. Before we closed and handed over the keys, the new owners came through with their contractor, planning to add the second bathroom we had never gotten around to building. The blueprints for the new addition hung on the door of the guest room like a scarlet letter.

Leaving home, letting go, was in some way my variation on self-flagellation. It was a relinquishing of control, a self-inflicted punishment. I had to leave in order to wipe the slate clean, but also to prove my asceticism. To prove I could live without comfort, without the totems I had gathered around me to signify my arrival as a functional adult. They were arbitrary. And without Lev, they were meaningless.

⊶————⊷

When we were children, my parents told my younger brother and me that we could pick which of their religions we wanted to join. My father is a secular man, raised an observant Jew. Spent of his patience with ritual, he married an Episcopalian: my mother, a private woman, never one to discuss her political leanings or religious inclination with her children or with anyone. Neither of my parents—at any point—spoke to me of a higher power in which I could or should believe. Perhaps each assumed that I—as an outgrowth of my precociousness—had badgered someone else into illuminating for me the concept of God and creation and the afterlife and how to live well on earth. It seemed to me that both of them were, at best, lukewarm on the whole business of worship. Certainly, they were not fervent. As it was, no one introduced me to the holy, to reverence, to the infinite. I never did believe in God. Instead I found comfort in superstition, in gut feelings, in coincidence and connection, in magnetism.

In the months before Lev was born and in the months surrounding his death, I accepted prayers on his behalf. I coveted them. I didn't believe they were going to a God who would hear and answer them, but I was moved by the desire of the faithful to make them. I was taken with the idea that friends and neighbors and congregations of strangers in faraway suburbs were thinking of my child and wishing him well. I was moved by their collective belief, which I envied and respected. The resonance of their devotion felt powerful. That these people cared for Lev and our family and that they wanted their God to know it was a wonder to me. Their prayers were something in which I could have faith. After Lev died, my husband—who had always been spiritual—dove headlong into religion. He began attending synagogue regularly and embarked on Torah study with the rabbi who'd memorialized Lev. My husband's sudden and genuine commitment to Judaism, to organized religion, to God, served to affirm my certainty that there was no saving us.

•————•

The house in which I grew up sits across the street from a church, a lovely gray stone building where I attended nursery school a few days a week (the other days, I went to nursery school in a synagogue across town). On Sunday mornings, as a child, I'd watch the crowds of Methodists assemble and disperse through the great wooden doors. I especially loved it when there was a wedding and I could treat my front steps as bleachers for the big event. I'd wait there, sometimes for hours, for the bride to emerge in her gown, holding her flowers, beaming. I believed in love without anyone ever explaining it to me. I always believed in love.

I felt something approaching religious devotion toward the romantic ideal. I worshipped the twin idols of chemistry and human connection. In those moments when the world stops and you and the object of your ardor are the only people left in it, I glimpsed the sacred. Bed was my church, my refuge. I fell in love and in lust with saintly fervor. But in love, like everywhere else, I fought ghosts. I am not easily swayed from the path I want to be on, one I believe to be the right path, even if it's aiming me straight off a cliff. I had been so lost for so long. In the haze of summer, there were decisions to be made, things to be worked out. The fog was lifting. I had glimpsed a light.

HAIL MARY

I am a teenager in love. Even nearer to forty than thirty, this remains a basic truth about me. I thrive on the wet-eyed breathlessness of the beginning, on daydreaming about the moment when we'll next be together, the sensation that the air has been sucked from the room when things go sideways, the mental machinations of trying to right the wrongs—to fix it. These things take over my life when I'm in their grip. This teenage feeling is as much a part of me as the triangular scar on my knee from where I fell, otherwise uneventfully, when I was three. This is the heart of me.

A dozen years ago, while living in L.A., I came down with a terminal crush on a blond, tattooed, like-minded boy. I was twenty-five. He was twenty-six and hard partying but romantically fifteen, just like me. As it happened, we had a short affair that turned alchemically into an enduring friendship. When we'd talk after one or another of our relationships flamed out, he would tell me: "I'm waiting for the fairy tale. It's out there. I know it is . . ." After I'd gotten divorced, after Lev was gone, after I'd fallen in love again, I traveled to California to attend this blond boy's wedding. His hair was gray by then, as was mine under the mahogany dye. Over the years, he'd nursed my broken hearts, supported me, played with my kids, and drank whiskey with me at my kitchen table. On the day of his marriage, I wondered if he'd found the fairy tale or if, in the end, he'd committed to something more earthbound. He wouldn't say. He would never kiss and tell.

I'd never much longed for the stuff of fairy tales. Everything in love felt imaginary to me anyhow. The solipsist in me had written both parts of entire relationships that ebbed and flowed and raged untempered in my head, the actual relationships being far less important to either of us than I'd imagined them. I wrote open letters to the men with whom I was entangled. Nothing I wrote would I ever send, of course, but I'd keep writing in an effort to discern how in the hell to end the storyline of a thing that had never really started. I didn't want a literary love. I was in search of something scientific, a love as stable as the noble gases, the most reliably calm section of the periodic table. I imagined a love as light as helium and bright as neon—a love based in chemistry, not children's stories.

The first summer after the last with Lev was my undoing and my remaking.

At the end of the last summer, we'd taken the children to Montauk. Shambled marriage and cancer be damned, we would take comfort in the yearly ritual of our trip east. We ate oysters and lobsters plucked straight from the water. We drank wine in the garden and closed our eyes against the bright sun. In the photos, Lev eats fresh blueberries from a metal mixing bowl and smiles big at whoever's taking the picture. The boys played together on the lawn in the dry-docked kayak and in the sand at the rocky bay beach. We suspended the inevitable; believed everything was okay, would be okay.

The summer after, we brought our only boy to the beach again. Like before. Like always. For Independence Day fireworks, for swimming in the ocean and cordial games of Scrabble. We furloughed our sadness. We slept in separate bedrooms. We got drunk together and discussed the demise of our relationship in fancy hotel patio bars. Everything was okay. After the holiday, I left for Texas while Joss stayed behind for a long vacation with his father and grandmother. On the jitney to the airport, I reread *Gatsby*.

———•

I spent the flight from Long Island home to Austin contemplating all of the messes. The smallest of which was how I would get back to my house from the airport. As of my layover, there were no takers. None had yet materialized by the time the plane landed. I stood in baggage claim, marshalling my cargo for a cab ride when in came a text from the iconoclast. He was on his way to fetch me. This kindness was, in itself, all kinds of unprecedented. Our relationship fit between the cracks, and so that's where it lived. The nature of the thing was arms-length and low-maintenance. We didn't do many (or any) favors for one another. Asking him for a ride from the airport had been a last resort. I hadn't expected him to oblige. Had I? I don't know if I was exactly happy that he had. Or perhaps I was elated. I put on lip gloss and dragged my suitcase to the curb to wait. Back at my place, in the quiet, air-conditioned afternoon, I took my mess to bed. It was a Wednesday. Eleven days before Lev's birthday.

Of all of my messes, the iconoclast was the most teen-aged of all. I had been first infatuated with the iconoclast for years. And then I'd thought I loved him. He loved me back, I was pretty sure. Or I thought, maybe. It was complicated. I'd known him forever. He had held sway over some part of me since long before I'd met my husband or the blond tattooed boy. He'd once described his feelings for me in the way I'd described the ticking of a woman's biological clock. Like baby fever. He couldn't stop himself, no matter how inconvenient, no matter how ill-advised. He was compelled. Compelled by biology. But no matter how much affection there was between us, he would never say he loved me. Perhaps he didn't love me. He never once said he did.

I'd never asked the iconoclast for anything. I'd never wanted anything more than what we had. But in the summer, it became not enough. Or it was too much. He felt the change coming; tried to head it off. He insisted everything could stay the same. That his place in my life could stay the way it was no matter what, even if there was someone else who became important to me. He was wary. Bordering on jealous. I sighed. Kissed him. And explained. I explained to him that in matters of love I had always been intense and single-minded and that my grief had distilled these qualities, made them even more so. That I was all or nothing now, and that there wasn't space for anyone else with him taking up so much of me. I couldn't break away to figure things out yet. I wasn't ready. But I needed to figure things out. I was all or nothing. And this was almost all and almost nothing at once.

I spent the night before Lev's birthday out with friends, happy. There was a dog at the bar. I danced. And there was a kiss. A kiss it would take me months to figure out. It knocked me into someplace new; calmed me, made me want to stay quiet and listen. I listened. One night, on my way to tell jokes at an open mic, I heard. I heard it over the sound of myself singing at the top of my voice. As I sang I knew. It was love. I was giddy. I was dumb. Stupid love. I was in love. Irrefutable love. I had never felt anything approaching this feeling ever, never in my whole life. Oh man, love.

Five days after Lev's birthday, the iconoclast and his girl left for their summer vacation, during which he would celebrate his fortieth birthday. The day before they left, we lay on his couch and made out a while. He cried when he read the birthday card I wrote him. I cried a little too. For his trip, I left him a mixtape, my final awkward stab at explaining—using other people's words—exactly how I felt about him, about us, about all of it . . .

The Hail Mary Pass

Track 1—"This Tornado Loves You" (Neko Case)

Track 2—"Flying on the Ground Is Wrong" (Neil Young)

Track 3—"Shell Games" (Bright Eyes)

Track 4—"It's Late" (Queen)

Track 5—"Brass in Pocket" (Pretenders)

Track 6—"Crazy About You" (Ryan Adams & Whiskeytown)

Track 7—"Pick Up the Change" (Wilco)

Track 8—"West Coast" (Coconut Records)

Track 9—"Animal" (Miike Snow)

Track 10 —"I Want You Back" (Jackson 5)

Track 11—"St. Elsewhere" (Gnarls Barkley)

Track 12—"Hurricane Glass" (Catherine Feeny)

Track 13—"White Blank Page" (Mumford & Sons)

Track 14—"Skinny Love" (Bon Iver)

Track 15—"Laughing with a Mouth of Blood" (St. Vincent)

Track 16—"Make You Feel My Love" (Adele)

Track 17—"George Michael" (One More Try)

Track 18—"You Don't Know Me" (Ben Folds)

That afternoon would be the last time for us although I didn't know it then. By the time the iconoclast returned from his trip, I had found the distance I needed to break orbit.

●————●

I fell in love for the first time when I was thirty-six. Of course, I thought I had been in love before. But I don't suppose I had. When I finally fell, I had been married for a decade and divorced. We'd lost our tiny son to a devastating illness that took three years to kill him. My marriage ended in that way where everything just melts and fades like it's been left in a hot car, the destructive force too relentless to fight and exhausting in its certainty. I'd had my heart broken so many times I had been rendered unafraid and fully divested of hope and faith of any kind. And then: love.

I know now what I want. I want the rightmost column of the periodic table, elementally calm and bright and lighter than air. I want this thing I have now. I want to make it coffee and talk about France. I want to get up and write about it all day. I want to make more of it. Build a nest for it. Keep it safe. I want nothing to do with expectations. I want everything to do with love. Love is what I want. And I have it. I have all that I want right now.

THE THINGS I'VE KEPT

The morning of the night Lev died, I woke up early in his hospital room in the pediatric ICU, where he had been for two days. Lev hadn't felt well overnight and, as a consequence, I hadn't slept to speak of. My temper was short that morning, my nerves fried. I wasn't especially anxious about what was to come, mostly because I had no idea. I powered through like always. I didn't know that day's sunrise would mark the last one I would have two living children. I didn't treat it specially. I was at the edge of a cliff, but I didn't yet know it. And then Lev died. And I fell.

●━━━●

In a wooden bowl on the top of my dresser, nestled among cocktail rings and loose change, lives Lev's plastic hospital name bracelet from the day he was born. It's always been there, since I carried it home in my pocket. And there it stays . . .

On the morning Lev was born, I knew approximately what was coming. After examining from all angles the problems inherent in birthing a baby whose heart was plumbed backwards, we had settled on a planned induction two days before my due date to remove as many variables from the equation as possible. I had an appointment at 6:30 a.m. to have my water broken. I woke up a wreck. Bereft. I rode the ten minutes to the hospital in the passenger seat; in the dark of the pre-sunrise; in tears.

We'd tracked Lev's heart defects at prenatal cardiology appointments for months and I was frankly terrified of reaching the end of my pregnancy. The way it had been explained to us, Lev's heart defects would not be dangerous until after he was born. While he was in me, he was safe. I had everything he needed. As soon as I gave him over to the doctors, there was uncertainty. Chaos. They would whisk him away and make him medical. They would put him in an incubator and hook him to monitors. They would place IVs in him and deliver medications. They would, of course, do their best to save his life, to keep him safe. And then they would set in motion their plan to cut him open and rearrange his tiny heart parts. After he was out of me, I could only wait. For months I would sit in rooms, waiting for news, and hope the prayers of the faithful held weight in the balance of the universe.

At 12:30 in the afternoon on July 16, 2007, after a short four hours of labor, I delivered Lev in a fully equipped operating room packed with capable medical strangers. There were no complications. After he was out of me, they put my new son on my chest and I got to see his chubby face and beautiful red hair for a few seconds before they whisked him away and up to the NICU to be prepared for the fight. No matter how I might have wished it different, my son would now belong to the doctors until the point at which he lived or died. The next time I saw him, he was enclosed in the state-of-the-art transport Isolette. He looked to me like a

rare pheasant under glass. I could touch only his hand. I
didn't know it yet, but I would know him mostly like this
for the next four months. He left for the children's hospital
and I stayed behind at the hospital where he'd been born,
now in a tiny mother-baby room, a mother with no baby.
My legs were still numb from the epidural. Until I could
stand and walk, I was a prisoner in my bed. My husband
sent me cell phone photos and updated me periodically on
Lev's progress, but I was unsoothed, jealous of his proxim-
ity, frustrated that I couldn't touch Lev or hear him cry or
nurse him. My son—my tiny son who'd lived in my body
and should need me, but didn't—was hours old and miles
away. In my impotence, I became hormonally furious and
yelled at everyone I saw for reasons justified and not. I
sobbed myself to sleep. Taking into account all that would
come later, I can say—without reservation—the day Lev
was born was the saddest of my life.

In my kitchen, there's an orange steamer trunk contain-
ing Lev's shoes and his favorite books, his shirts and tiny

hats, a set of Tibetan prayer flags. There are the memorial cards from his funeral. There is his pacemaker. There are baby quilts and paper cranes and Lev's stuffed dog, who was called Ernie.

Lev's first birthday was mostly joyous. During our summer trip to Albany that year, we celebrated my dad's seventieth birthday and Lev's first birthday with a joint party for family and friends. It was lovely for everyone to finally meet the conquering hero. Though it was somewhat of a Pyrrhic victory we celebrated that day. Lev's torso was a map of scar tissue from heart surgeries and chest tubes and central lines. He was still fragile, on the razor's edge. He was on a regimen of meds and a rotation of therapies. He ate most of his diet through a feeding tube surgically implanted in his belly. In the night—every night—I would rush to his bedside to check if he was breathing. He was always fine, but I never exhaled.

The July Lev turned two, his right eye crossed. He'd started walking about seven days earlier and we were worried one of the spills he'd taken had jostled something vital. A few days before his birthday, we took him to the emergency room thinking better safe than sorry. They admitted him to the hospital overnight, but he was home in time for his party.

To fete the second birthday of the inexplicably cross-eyed lion, we had bouquets of balloons, tables piled high with home-cooked food, and a great tureen of watermelon agua-fresca. There was a blur of children running everywhere. Lev wore his green Converse high-tops. A friend made a sculpted birthday cake with colored polka dots of white chocolate fondant (so beautiful one could have entered it in a contest, if one did that sort of thing). In my very favorite photo of Lev, taken on this day, he has his head thrown back, his eyes closed in laughter. In the slightly soft-focus black-and-white photo, you can't see the mysterious crossed eye that was misdiagnosed over a period of months as a symptom of a bone infection, as the result of cranial nerve palsy, and eventually as the sign of a benign tumor for which we scheduled surgery in the fall. It was when they opened him up on that cool, late October morning that they finally discovered the brain cancer. The surgeon saw it with his naked eyes, everywhere, all over Lev's brain, brazen. It had been there all along. At Lev's second birthday party, we didn't know a thing. We ate cake.

To mark Lev's third birthday, we had a party in the park adjacent to the hospital where we'd spent most of the preceding year waiting for the scales to tip. Lev had battled cancer for eight of the previous twelve months. He was weary and circumspect that day, a warrior at rest. And although he was home from the front for the moment, to look at him was not to gaze upon triumph. Half of his face still drooped, a lingering effect of the surgeries to remove the tumors. A long red scar snaked around one of his ears and across his head, shouting through the sparse straw-blond hair that had barely begun to grow back.

The mid-July heat was mean that afternoon—over 100 degrees and not at all bearable, close and damp and cruel as hell. It made us quiet. My parents, a handful of our friends, and the teachers from Lev's special needs preschool came out to celebrate. The weather and presumably the sadness kept everyone else away. The heat was so oppressive on

the day of Lev's party the guests mostly sat in the shade
or stood still, leaning against fixed objects. Joss and the
other kids played with Lev's new lawn bowling set and
squirted each other with water bottles. They seemed to
have a good time. We all ate slowly from deli sandwich
trays and communal bags of chips and drank juice boxes.
There was a cupcake-cake from the grocery store with
whipped-cream frosting that wilted and melted and slid
off the cakes. The party was short.

Next to my bed, on a lacquered tray painted with silver
birds, sits the striped zebrawood urn inside which Lev's
dust quietly settles. There is a scattering of other objects
on the tray, arranged shrine-like: a candle in a glass hurricane, a turquoise floral book of matches, a set of three
framed portraits of the boys, and beside the urn a smaller
box that used to hold fancy French chocolates. Inside the
chocolate box are the cake toppers from Lev's third and
final birthday cake: three cheap plastic Elmo figurines.
Prized possessions.

The year after Lev died, I was alone on his birthday, by design. Joss was in Montauk with his dad. My parents were in Albany. My friends were at arm's length. I didn't know if I would wake up on that morning feeling like the madwoman in the attic or like a robot or like whatever might lie between those two poles. I felt it all. That day, more than any other, I fancied myself a rōnin, a solitary soldier in service to a ghostly lion prince. I wandered my apartment absently abandoning cups of tea and plates of food, my phone alerting me all the while as the texts and emails came in commemorating the day. I went out and paid someone for another cup of tea, drove myself to an appointment at a spa—which seemed like a good idea at the time—and I sat placidly through the various treatments and pampering. I can't say I felt any comfort, but it felt right. Afterward, I read a message from my dad and I sat in my car and wept. I forgot to breathe at one point. I'd held my breath without realizing it until I started to feel faint. Then I went shopping. I bought a few pretty things: a striped blouse, some sparkly earrings, and perfume that smelled, to me, like bright future (really like bay rum and orange blossoms). I drank a glass of wine. A friend took me out for diner food and a terrible movie. I went to sleep content.

This was the first of Lev's birthdays where I wasn't terrified, where I wasn't paralyzed in some way by the looming end. The war was over. We'd been beaten. On that day, my grief was prismatic. I could see in every direction—all of the things that had come before, each of the paths not chosen. And I could see everything possible. Lev is gone. But in leaving, he made all of the possible futures. In all of them, I'm falling. The good news is there is no ground.

•————•

On the table by the front door in my apartment, there's a framed photo of me holding Lev at age two, taken in the backyard of the cottage in Montauk. He's looking at the camera; I'm looking at him. Both of us are laughing. These are the things I've kept. The rest of all of it is inside me, waiting to stay or go, to get lost or be written.

THE SCARLET *D*

If marriage were easy, or even if being married was roughly what one thought it would be like, every couple would stay married until death parted them. But, of course it isn't; statistically, marriage is a fifty-fifty gamble. Perhaps I should find some comfort in the sheer number of other folks for whom being husband and wife has proven unsustainable, but I don't. I don't, because in the end I failed. We failed. We failed to make each other happier than sad. We failed to want to make it work. We failed to keep the vows we made. Vows we found on the internet and said in front of our families and friends, and in front of the judge who married us. (A judge, incidentally, who was divorced and remarried. We chose this judge because I used to babysit for his daughter—from his first marriage—when I was in high school.)

My husband filed for divorce ten days after Lev died, coincidental with the radioactive meltdown of the life we'd built. In the days between Lev's death and when our divorce proceedings began, we had sat together and picked out an urn for Lev's dust. We'd driven together on the morning of the funeral during which he'd held my arm firmly and with care so that I would not crumple as our son was eulogized. In these moments, I relaxed into the realization that this man whom I did not love anymore was, in fact, a devoted father, a nurturer, and someone on whom I could rely to take thoughtful care of our son. (This both comforted and confused me. Where was this man in the years when our children were tiny, when I felt lost and overwhelmed and it was all I could do not to drown in a sea of need and the feeling that there was never enough? If he'd shown himself then, would things be different now?) After the mourners left, I resumed squatting in my parent's condo with very few of my things or Joss's things. Each and every time I drove to the house to retrieve some sort of belonging that felt important, my blood pressure rose. And so, after the essentials were squirreled away in my new nest, I stayed away. There was fallout. There were macabre imitations of happy holidays: our first Thanksgiving and Hanukkah and Christmas without Lev were each horror revues of epic scope, full to the brim with awkward moments and well-meaning whole folk who served to reflect our shatteredness.

I think he filed for divorce because I said I wanted it, which I did. I'd insisted there was absolutely no turning back, and yet I'd made no move toward the reality of getting divorced. In the end, he knew me better than I might have liked to admit. His filing was both a chess move and a careful nudge: *This is real; we're doing this.* My husband of approximately ten years knew well that I have a tendency to become paralyzed at life's crossroads—to dig my heels into confusion or misery or terror and close my eyes until it's over and/or until someone has made a decision for me. Trying to grieve without dying myself, to get up each day and not lose my shit, to parent separately in two homes, took all I had. I had nothing left for the logistics of dissolving a marriage. At the point when I clamped my eyes shut, covered my ears, and shook my head against the responsibility of finishing either my marriage or my divorce, I'd coasted through a decade relying on my husband to make the difficult driving decisions of our relationship. He was keenly aware of this cultivated weakness of mine. And so, as it happened, even though it was I who had thrown down the gauntlet and declared our marriage to be over, it was he who had filed for divorce, he who hired a lawyer, and he who saw the process through until it was done.

Over the decade we'd spent as a couple—though we'd wanted to keep things together, tried to cover our bases as we pursued our diverging interests—we'd behaved badly in times of crisis. I suppose we'd not had the maturity or the coping skills to treat each other well. Grudges were held; bonds eroded. Our marriage limped on, if only just barely, through many chances to stay or go. In the end, most of our trespasses against one another were brought to bear. Knowing the details of each other's base ugliness left us with a coldness, an incredulity at how far off the golden path we'd traveled. We'd devolved into unpredictable strangers who'd known each other well a long time ago, but not anymore.

In the state of Texas, if both parties want it, it's not particularly complicated or time-consuming to get divorced. File some paperwork, wait sixty days, file more paperwork, and boom—you're divorced. Although it could have been this simple, the official legal split did not go so quickly or easily for us. In the end, our very mutual divorce dragged. By the time i's were dotted and t's were crossed on the legal document dissolving our union, we had been living apart for a purgatorial year. During that nebulous time, there was my husband's pilgrimage to Israel. There was bullshit. There were my attempts to regroup in Albany, in St. Louis, in Los Angeles. There was dating for both of us. There was psychology and psychiatry. There was renewed fighting and forced mediation before there was peace. There was the sale of our house and the exhaustive preparations that presaged it. There was Joss's first day of kindergarten. There was love. Everything—as ever—was impossible and possible and happening.

One morning in September, I woke up to a call from my husband (followed shortly by an email from his attorney) telling me our divorce had been finalized and granted. And that was that. I went to work, Joss went to school, it was as anticlimactic as a thing that life-changing could be. Though we had been by all rights over for years, I had expected to feel more of a punch to the stomach when I became marriage status: Divorced. But instead, I bore the scarlet *D* with calmness. I'd earned it fair and square.

As I settle into the unfamiliar calmness of this next, sweet phase of my life, I'm happy and in love and writing and living alone (with son) for the first time ever in my life. I feel lucky. And I am so very grateful. I'm grateful for my ex-husband's wholehearted embrace of parenting, for his delight at being Joss's dad. We are and always will be Joss's family. Throwing in the towel as spouses made us that much more determined to take the one unassailably good thing left of our relationship and elevate it beyond reproach. To continue the détente we needed to be equal parents to our son (on whose tiny shoulders our legacy now rests), we needed to keep moving forward, to not get stuck in some terrible resentful place—a common place, the worst place—where fingers are pointed and no one wins. We've committed to be gentle to one another in service to the happiness of our remaining son (who has been through enough and does not need his parents' petty bullshit raining acid down on his life). I'm grateful for my ex-husband taking control and seeing our divorce through, for his being even-tempered enough to realize that this was the only way forward, even though it maybe wasn't always what he wanted. I am grateful that, after all of the shit we put one another through, he still loved me enough to finish what I'd started. He let me go.

THE VESSEL

My ex-husband postulated once in the context of a fight near the end of our marriage that maybe deep down I was broken, wired only for sadness. The idea that I was incapable of being happy shut me right up. Mostly because I had thought the same thing myself and was pretty sure this made it true. Without question, I'd long since put my head down into the wind and ceased trying to find any sort of joy. I was hard and mean. I had broken my husband's heart and made him hate me. Lev was gone, my marriage was over, my house belonged to someone else. There was no denying I was deeply and corrosively unhappy. In doing what I'd needed to do to stay alive, I'd gone dark. I saw the shadow in advance of the sun. I functioned in a state of relentless angry discontent. I didn't mince words. I made hard decisions. And if you got in my way, I took you down. I knew, from experience, things would likely get worse before and if they would ever get better. I learned to manage my despondence, to box it up and move forward. I had no expectation of ever being happy, but I suppose I needed not to be exactly this unhappy.

I'd been effortlessly happy once. I can remember the remote feeling of falling in love, of gazing at the faces of my babies as they slept in my arms, of sitting on the porch of our first home in Los Angeles drinking tea and staring out over downtown feeling like I'd bought the whole world. And just as vividly, I remember losing my grip on my marriage, kissing Lev's forehead after he'd died, leaving the house at the top of the hill and running from L.A. to Texas after I'd miscarried our first baby and I'd begun to spiral out of control. My happiness was brief and bound always to its opposite.

I found I had no coping skills for sustained contentment. I was grateful to rest there awhile, but could never make it stick. The idea that I (or anyone) would need to cope with happiness—as opposed to embracing and rolling with it—strikes me as a touch deranged. But that was exactly it. I had worn deep grooves of worry and sadness into the surface of my brain. I had rewired things for ease of misery. It felt comfortable, if not pleasant, in the sad bits, something like wearing mean shoes where you've taped over all of the blister-y spots but the ache remains inescapable. I had spent so many years with my face held to a fire, with my eyes downcast, with my shoulders hunched, I had forgotten how to feel well. Instead of lightening my load, happiness tripped me—a pebble underfoot.

.

At my lowest ebb, I busied myself with feverishly eavesdropping on the lives of others—certain theirs was the stuff of envy. I sought examples of happiness, models for living, for how it was done. There's a whole wide world within the world. One where everyone's reduced to an amalgamation of images and statuses, alone behind screens, lurking in the shadows of old news and expired relationships, consumed with the need to prove joie de vivre to everyone and no one in particular. I thought, in watching lives unfold in scrolling text and photos, I might find just the happy examples I craved. Watching became a compulsion for me. Each boy that broke my heart, each friend who left my life, I watched to see where their path took them after it diverged from mine. I wanted to judge their comings and goings, to critique their new friends, to feel like I was somehow still connected to their future, if only as an observer. Each woman I knew who had two healthy children, each younger person who was just falling in love, each older person happily married for decades . . . they had figured it out and I was flailing. I watched them, hoping to find clues to their success. Or I watched them in the hope they would stumble so I could feel better. I watched them and hoped that they were watching me too and that my life—when viewed as a series of carefully curated updates and photos and links to pop-culture memes and videos of adorable animals—looked better than it really was.

I found, one day in my virtual travels, the story of a woman buried for 2,500 years high in the frozen mountains of Siberia. Near the end of the twentieth century, archaeologists uncovered her mummified remains. She was twenty-five years old when she died and heavily tattooed with inks of black and red in the shape of animals and mystical symbols. She'd been buried with a retinue of horses and warrior guards in full regalia. It's unclear if she was of the noble class—an actual princess—or if she might have been an especially important storyteller: a woman of magic. The idea that those two stations might be of interchangeable importance seemed right to me, and it resonated. I'm neither royal nor magic, but I am a story-teller, tattooed and fierce. I don't know yet what they'll say about me, only that I won't know how it ends. And I know the story won't be written on my Facebook wall.

The realm of the virtual presented the opposite of a model for living. I found, instead, a model for yearning. I needed to get the fuck out. I had to meet real people, to ask them questions and to listen to the answers. I had to make a life. In the dark year of days between my thirty-sixth and thirty-seventh birthdays, I began. I let the vessel of Lev's absence lead me out into the unceasingly vast, miasmic ocean of all possible things. The careening quality of this year was intense and constant. Out of control lost with no great desire to be found. My losses cast a dim darkness over what lay ahead: a twilight that might have signaled dusk or dawn. Technically speaking, there are three kinds of twilight. There is civil twilight—where objects earthly and celestial are visible. There is astronomical twilight— where the blackness of the sky is rich and full of stars. And then there is nautical twilight, during which the horizon becomes blurred and one cannot see to properly navigate. Such was the half-light of my darkest year, hazy and indistinct and difficult—but not impossible—to negotiate.

I set out alone. I abandoned my hairdresser, my dentist, my primary care doctor. I was raw nervous grief walking. I couldn't stomach the thought of sitting in pneumatic chairs with familiar strangers having my teeth cleaned or my hair styled, my parts examined, feeling pressure to explain to nice folks—who were just doing their jobs and did not need their day ruined—that my son had died. I was restless and noncommittal for months and went through several iterations of grooming and healthcare professionals before I felt like I could sit still and just be in the moment with our collective sadness. I let everything go to seed in the process. I changed the color of my hair in my bathroom at home using materials bought at Wal-Mart. I neglected my gums.

My memories of the months between Lev's first posthumous birthday and the anniversary of his death are lush and buttery and vividly colored. The final reel of my darkest year, comprised of the 106 days between Lev's birthday and mine, is in soft focus watercolors—frames of a dream directed by Sofia Coppola. I am the happiest I've ever been. I had spent the year casually dating and discarding more and better men than any one woman deserved, but I was done now. I had no unresolved crushes or old loves for whom I still pined. I had not let myself run from this something real. I was holding steady at calm and quiet.

When happiness came, it knocked me on my ass and nearly killed me. I swooned and almost passed out in a burger joint on an August morning. Between Lev's birthday and mine, I had five cavities filled—the first cavities of my life. When Joss wasn't with me I kept nothing in the fridge except champagne and the makings of a fruit and cheese plate. I ate candy for lunch. I developed crazy high blood pressure and ended up, briefly, in the emergency room on a Monday when I was supposed to be in therapy. For the hypertension, I took medication that made me feel hot and sleepy, but never better. I was sick and tired and skinny with weird hair and rotting teeth but I was breathlessly happy.

When Lev was born, he lived in the hospital for 113 days before he was well enough to come home. The grinding days between Lev's birthday and the day he became ours for real were filled with more disappointment than respite, more scars than anyone could count. We brought him home for the first time on November 6, 2007. Each of the years Lev was alive, I crawled through the stretch between his birthday and November 6, associating those months with our collective worry, with dodging death and waiting to live. Each year, as the in-between days crept by, I relived the wondering what I would do if I never got to take him home and I began what would become a ritual of praying in my way that I could get to keep him for a little while longer. That first year, and each year he lived, on November 6, I allowed myself to exhale. In the end,

Lev left us on November 3—three days shy of the day he first came home; four days after my thirty-sixtth birthday; three years and 110 days after the day he was born. I count the days to assign some sense of order to the great jumbled clod of them, but really, they're just and simply days, each one the same: each one devastating and fine.

On the night before my thirty-seventh birthday, I ate a big Italian meal, just like I did every year of my childhood. I went to bed sated and full. My birthday, October 30, we celebrated with decadent Sunday breakfast for a table full of friends at a restaurant we reserve for halcyon days. Halloween is next, with costumes for Joss, then All Saints Day and All Souls Day. Finally, on November 3, the anniversary of his death, those of us who loved him mark Lev's day. On that day I will be busy. I will pick my mother up at the airport and visit my storage space to retrieve the single box into which I'd packed the most precious of Lev's things. On that day, I will feel pain. I have an appointment to get a tattoo of Lev's initial. Considering the collection of ink already illustrating me, the new addition will be a tiny flourish, a bookend. I will be lucky. In the evening, a friend has arranged for tickets to see Joan Rivers, an idol of mine since forever. When I meet Ms. Rivers after the show, she will be so tiny I will think maybe I could fit her in my purse. When I say this out loud, she will look at me like I'm crazy. It will be strange and wonderful. I will drink Scotch and Irish whiskey that night and I will fall into bed with gusto, dizzy and in love with everything. This feeling won't end. It will stretch on and on for miles and ages into the horizon. It's all only just beginning.

I hope when they find me someday, buried in ice, they unravel my story and the ending is beautiful.

EPILOGUE

I am consumed most moments by a feeling of sham adulthood, of profound adolescence. Always a late bloomer, I'm dubious as to whether this re-teenaged state in which I find myself is a function of grief and renewal or whether I'm just now finding my way for the first time, admitting that I was never really all that grown-up. Of one thing, I am certain: I am not the person I was before Lev died. Nor am I the person I was at the end of the first year, the 365 collected days of which, I was supported, carried, sometimes to the point of feeling suffocated—childlike. I became very nearly the ward of my wider world and filled with some kind of crazy uncharacteristic peace and faith in the universe, never alone by accident and never alone by choice.

In year two, the world went back about its business. Lev's tiny legend faded. The well-meaning sympathy of acquaintances soured into something like pity. People listened a little less patiently when I talked about sad things. A feeling of otherness crept on me and fogged me all up, shut me down. I stopped talking about Lev so much. I began to make choices when meeting new people, whether to tell them about Lev at all. I need to decide within a few moments of meeting someone if I want to know that person beyond our introduction. And if I do, I must then find the words to explain my loss and how it's going to be okay. They need to know it's going to be okay, so I tell them it will be. I can tell the whole story of Lev's life quickly and without crying, with a smile, even. But it doesn't get easier. It never gets any easier. More often, when meeting new people, I tell them I have just one child (a child with an implied unremarkable medical history). They don't need to know all about me. Lev gets redacted in the interest of everyone's comfort.

For five years, I've shown up to work every day in a beautiful, world-class children's hospital. I have a unique unicorn of a job advising the hospital on the experience of being a parent of a patient, working with medical professionals at the top of their respective games, people who are the best in their field at healing children. We work together every day to figure out how to build a better mousetrap from the inside out. I work with men and women of all stripes, from housekeepers to hospital executives to doctors and everyone in between. My job was challenging while Lev was living—switching hats between mother and employee, between problem and solution. Talking with the doctors at Lev's bedside about his heart medication and pacemaker settings and cancer treatment and then meeting those same doctors at boardroom tables to talk about construction projects and hospital policy changes. Sleeping in Lev's room at night and tumbling bleary down to my office in the morning to host family coffee hours for parents of patients, to learn their stories, to feed them back to the system. I used to tell pieces of my story to help parents contextualize the experience of having a sick baby. I was just like them. With Lev gone, I'm two years into my role as the worst-case scenario. As the mother of a child who couldn't be saved, I am a constant reminder of what no one likes to remember: you can't win them all. I'm a casualty of the wider war—a shambled diplomat. I am the ambassador of a devastated country whose name we don't say. Gone from the map. I smile and nod and listen and ask questions. I don't tell my story to the parents anymore.

In the first year after Lev died, the ladies who worked the cafeteria check-out line would occasionally catch me off guard by asking how I was holding up, how my parents were doing, or telling me they missed seeing my sweet boy. Once and again they would tell me their own stories of grief and ask my advice in solidarity. I'd feel bad in these moments that I didn't know all of their names. I didn't know anything about them. But they knew me. And they'd known my son. They knew the sad ending to our story: my son died of cancer and heart disease in a room one floor up from where they serve lunch; one floor down from the gift shop. He died just down the hall from the sunny courtyard where he'd met his brother for the first time three years earlier. He died in a bed a short elevator ride from my office where I'm about to eat a four-dollar salad for lunch. Thank you. Have a nice day.

———

One month to the day before Lev died, I was at a friend's baby shower in Los Angeles. The hosts of the shower arranged the services of a tarot card reader for the party. The guests were abuzz. When the ersatz soothsayer arrived, she looked to be in costume. Dressed in striped thigh-highs and a tutu, her hair in pigtails, she approximated a stripper version of a circus sideshow gypsy: clownish without winking, a performer. The filmy veil of artifice, an extension of the one that mostly envelops my beloved L.A., made me tired on top of tired. No need to make a party trick of predicting my future. My path was clear. The day before the shower, Lev's doctors had confirmed a relapse of cancer, and I spent much of that happy day hiding on the sun porch, trying to keep it together, crying dryly on the phone with Lev's dad. I'd been ruminating on a way out of ruminating. I knew our story had an end, but I didn't want to see it quite so clearly.

At the alarm of the relapse diagnosis, I woke up to what Lev faced. I hadn't known I was sleeping, but I had been fast asleep, complacent. Facing the universal truth—just because a lot of bad shit happens to a person doesn't stop more bad shit from coming—helped to put everything in line. The dam between the present and the next place had burst. A river of shit was coming for us harder and faster, nowhere to go but under. I demurred on the tarot reading. I flew back to Austin early the next morning to begin the end run.

After Lev died and the rushing stopped, I took comfort in the idea that life without Lev might be something like filling a cargo ship with experiences, like a treasure hunt; sailing the blue-green ocean of all-things-possible. The image became a totem for me: my life as a boat with Lev as its captain. The first year after Lev's death, I bobbed along drowsily in this gently waved and salt-scented dream. I wasn't particularly curious about the future. I was hungry for it, ready for all of it. I took it as it came. I began to write again and I chronicled year one in a bubble of self-reflection and gratitude, reveling in possibility and potential.

The second year was different. Murky. My vessel felt exactly like a spacecraft hurtling through the blackness of infinity, of possibility to the nth degree. Too dark for me to see a way forward, propelled to the next place by physics I didn't understand, I faced the permanence of the loss I'd experienced. The future was a nebula. A vacuum. The void. This is Major Tom to ground control. I'm stepping through the door. And I'm floating in a most peculiar way. And the stars look very different today.

Two full years out from Lev's death, I feel lost. Which is to say, I feel like myself again: armored, dukes up. I'm past the year of firsts—first birthdays and holidays and anniversaries post-Lev are all past. Everything is old or brand new. Nothing has more meaning than it should. Yet, nothing about Lev's absence has lessened for me with the passage of time. I don't know that I expected my grief to grow smaller, but perhaps I hoped it would grow more manageable. More stable. If anything, living with the pain longer has meant more pain, compounded pain. But one becomes accustomed to the feeling of living with ghosts, gets used to being haunted. I dread the day, soon, when

Lev will have been dead longer than he was alive, when I will have lived longer with his ghost than I did with my darling boy.

In the second half of my second year without Lev, I met a woman I'd previously known by reputation and admired, a true renaissance woman—a character and an open book. A doyenne. A maven. An artist. A dealer in rare antiques. A woman of all these many talents and more. And yet she manages to be the opposite of intimidating, so warm you feel instantly that you've always known her. She and I met in the backyard of a dive bar and our rambling conversation touched on death and grief and love and grandiosity of all sorts. After we spoke, we corresponded for the better part of a year about various bits and dreams, half-heartedly planning to reconnect, life always intervening. We'd not yet found the time to have coffee or cordials or to gossip over steaks, but we knew we'd meet again. I'd long known that one of her trades was doing tarot card readings in a 1940s Spartanette trailer in the backyard of her rambling house. The inclination to have a reading done for myself had never so much as flickered, until suddenly—with my birthday and Lev's second deathiversary looming—I found myself seeking clarity with some mounting degree of desperation. Feeling humbled and hopelessly stuck, I was aflame with the need to gain some direction. It was time to close the loop. To feel focused on the future again, instead of always feeling the unrelenting suck of the past, I would face my fortune.

When I sat down with this lovely woman on my lunch break from the hospital, on a crisp and windy Friday afternoon, I felt nervous and teary and self-conscious. She poured me a glass of water and took my hands in hers and we began the series of rituals and careful shuffling choices that make up a reading of the tarot. She wore a head wrap and a sweater befitting the weather and giant claret-colored rope braid earrings that brushed her shoulders. She was not in costume. She was herself: one in a million. The reading she offered was full of parables and pragmatic interpretation, more like therapy than like a visit to a mystical realm. The array staring back at me was indisputably mine. She suggested I take a photo of the cards all laid out and so I did. The grief card, the hermit, the moon. Rulers and gifts. Wands upon wands. Swords upon swords. The practical and the silly and the divine. "Do this thing. Take these steps. The universe has gifts for you. It's all right here . . ." Year three.

•————•

I'm terrible at learning from the past. I make the same mistakes over and over. I wish could take everything that's happened and synthesize it into something great, something sage, some wisdom I can apply to parenting, to living, to love, to writing. I live with all of the decisions that made me, the choices that got me here to this place of alternating needless and needful worry, this place of adolescent rumination, of camping out inside my head doing nothing but damage. Right now, it all feels like a scrambled Rubik's Cube. I want to twist it into rightness, feel the parts click into place, see the colors line up. See them fall into order because I know how to fix it, not because I made the surface look right by switching the stickers. Believe me, I've tried. I learned a few things, though. I learned that aces are gifts from the universe. I learned it's easier to meditate with two swords than to hold three in your heart. I learned sad song lyrics are accurate predictors of how love will turn out in the end. I learned people are inherently good (except for assholes, who are everywhere). I learned that sometimes a job is a vocation and you do it despite the pain it causes you. And I learned where on the internet to find photos of firemen putting oxygen masks on kittens, because sometimes you need to remember that good things happen every day. Every day.

ACKNOWLEDGMENTS

I would like to thank Chris Monks and John Warner, my editors at *McSweeney's Internet Tendency*. Without Chris and John, these essays would be unwritten. To Cheryl Strayed, my North Star, I owe an immeasurable debt of gratitude. It was through Cheryl's editing of *The Best American Essays* that I met Megan Stielstra, who is part of my beating heart, and was so before we ever met. Megan, who, after a decade of friendship and three years of Zoom calls, willed this collection of mine into being at Northwestern University Press. Thank you, Megan, for being clutch and helping me to always find magic in the mess. To my amazing friends: you are my home. I love you all like Velveteen Rabbits. We are real and thread-bare together and there really is no other way I'd rather be. Thank you to my mom and dad, who still live in the house where my brother and I grew up, for being steadfast examples of how to keep going. And finally, thank you to my husband, the one and only boyfriend mentioned in any of these eighteen essays to make it all the way to the Big Show. Jason, I love you endlessly; all of the much.